Catastrophe and Conflict

AF714845

Catastrophe and Conflict

Disaster Diplomacy and Its Foreign Policy Implications

By

Ilan Kelman

BRILL

LEIDEN | BOSTON

Library of Congress Control Number: 2016930143

Want or need Open Access? Brill Open offers you the choice to make your research freely accessible online in exchange for a publication charge. Review your various options on brill.com/brill-open.

Typeface for the Latin, Greek, and Cyrillic scripts: "Brill". See and download: brill.com/brill-typeface.

ISBN 978-90-04-31613-3 (paperback)
ISBN 978-90-04-31614-0 (e-book)

Originally published as Volume 1(1) 2016, in *Diplomacy and Foreign Policy*, DOI 10.1163/24056006-12340001.

Copyright 2016 by Ilan Kelman. Published by Koninklijke Brill NV, Leiden, The Netherlands.
Koninklijke Brill NV incorporates the imprints Brill, Brill Hes & De Graaf, Brill Nijhoff, Brill Rodopi and Hotei Publishing.
Koninklijke Brill NV reserves the right to protect the publication against unauthorized use and to authorize dissemination by means of offprints, legitimate photocopies, microform editions, reprints, translations, and secondary information sources, such as abstracting and indexing services including databases. Requests for commercial re-use, use of parts of the publication, and/or translations must be addressed to Koninklijke Brill NV.

This book is printed on acid-free paper and produced in a sustainable manner.

Contents

Catastrophe and Conflict: Disaster Diplomacy and Its Foreign Policy Implications

Ilan Kelman
Institute for Risk & Disaster Reduction and Institute for Global Health, University College London, London, U.K.
Norwegian Institute of International Affairs, Oslo, Norway

Abstract

Disaster diplomacy examines how and why disaster-related activities (disaster response and disaster risk reduction) do and do not lead to diplomatic endeavours. With respect to foreign policy implications, the main question examined here is: Under what circumstances could disaster diplomacy be actively made to succeed or not succeed? Previous case studies are summarised followed by new case studies of disease diplomacy and climate change diplomacy. From the case studies, disaster diplomacy could succeed when those in power decide that they want it to succeed and then use their power for that goal. This situation is not likely to arise because of only disaster-related activities. Instead, pre-existing interests supporting diplomacy are needed.

Keywords

climate change – diplomacy – disaster – disaster risk reduction – disease – health

1 Prologue: Oceans Apart

On 26 December 2004, the largest earthquake to strike the planet in forty years shook the coastline off western Sumatra, Indonesia. At approximately 07:58:53 AM local time, at a location centring on 3.316°N and 95.854°E and about 30 km below the earth's surface, the shaking began, yielding a magnitude of 9.1–9.3, lasting 3–4 minutes, and rupturing along a fault length of 1,200–1,300 km and width of over 100 km (Lay et al., 2005; Park et al., 2005; USGS, 2015). The earthquake was felt over 1,000 km away in Bangkok. The earthquake shifted parts of the seafloor vertically by several metres, displacing a large amount of water and leading to a tsunami spreading out across the Indian Ocean.

At that time, no mechanism existed to issue a region-wide warning. Despite more than thirty years of previous efforts to set up an Indian Ocean tsunami warning system, it had not yet been done due to political decisions to avoid allocating funds (Kelman, 2006). Consequently, scientists analysing the real-time seismic data were left scrambling to try to issue ad hoc warnings during a holiday period in many of their countries and in many of the affected countries.

Many people had no warning or did not have enough time to respond. Within 30 minutes, the first tsunami deaths had occurred in Indonesia with the last casualties reported over seven hours later along Africa's east coast from South Africa to Somalia. As part of a total death toll of over 230,000 people in more than a dozen countries, citizens from more than thirty other countries were also killed.

In the meantime, some indigenous peoples in places such as Simeulue, Indonesia; the Nicobar and Andaman Islands, India; and coastal Myanmar knew that the shaking and their observations of the sea meant a tsunami was coming (Bishop et al., 2005; Dybas, 2005; Gaillard et al., 2008). Many evacuated and survived. Tourists in Thailand and Sri Lanka recognised some pre-tsunami signs leading to evacuations on their beaches which saved hundreds of lives (Cyranoski, 2005; Gregg et al., 2006).

In the end, the two worst-hit countries were Indonesia with over 130,000 people dead and Sri Lanka with over 35,000 people dead. Both countries had been embroiled in internal conflicts with a particularly high level of violence over the previous three decades. In Indonesia, Aceh was the worst-affected area and was in the midst of a separatist war with little access permitted by outsiders. The tsunami killed Indonesian soldiers as well as Acehnese separatists trapped in their prison cells. In Sri Lanka, the north and east areas of the island country were controlled by Tamils fighting the Sinhalese majority for independence, with civilians and other ethnic groups caught in the middle. Sri Lanka's east coast was particularly badly hit by the tsunami, with access controlled by the separatist fighters.

As the scale of the disaster around the Indian Ocean emerged—fuelled in part by the evocative disaster imagery from the disaster zones (Hutchinson, 2014)—the largest humanitarian relief operation up until that time swung into action. For relief supplies to reach affected locations and be distributed to people in need, Aceh and eastern Sri Lanka would need to be opened up to the outside world far more than they had been before. Hope was expressed that the need for humanitarian relief and post-tsunami reconstruction would help to resolve the conflicts.

Successful 'disaster diplomacy', a peace deal arising from a disaster, was discussed and, to a large degree, expected by the media and many humanitarian policy makers and practitioners. An assumption was made that warring parties would be driven together by the need to alleviate human suffering and then collaborate to effect assistance. Yet little evidence existed for this assumption. While it might be a human condition to strive for reconciliation efforts during times of difficulty, of which disaster diplomacy could be one example, it is important to have an evidence basis before assuming that this human condition would always exist and be acted upon.

As the results from Aceh and Sri Lanka show, hopes and expectations for disaster diplomacy were not fully met. The assumptions were wrong regarding automatic peace due to the humanitarian imperative. In fact, despite the parallels between both locations, the outcomes were vastly different.

Aceh, to a large extent, was opened up to the outside world. One month after the tsunami, on 23 January 2005, Acehnese fighters and the Indonesian government entered into peace talks in Helsinki. On 15 August 2005, a peace deal was signed. While problems did not disappear, with continuing low levels of violence and accusations of discrimination, the agreement has now held for more than a decade. Aceh resides firmly in a post-conflict, post-tsunami phase. On the surface, it appears to be successful disaster diplomacy.

Conversely, Sri Lanka's tsunami disaster was quickly used to exacerbate the conflict. In the tsunami-hit areas controlled by Sri Lanka's government, they delivered assistance including outside aid. In the Tamil-governed sectors, the fighters used their knowledge and control to respond immediately and to provide as much assistance as they could. Outside humanitarian aid was not immediately delivered to the Tamil-controlled areas because actions by authorities on both sides of the de facto internal border blocked it as part of a power struggle and asserting their authority over the disputed territory. Eventually, an agreement was reached in June 2005 regarding the distribution of aid to the Tamil-controlled locations. Sinhalese nationalists challenged the agreement in court on the constitutional basis that the authorities in the Tamil areas are terrorists and so should not be dealt with. Sri Lanka's Supreme Court upheld the challenge. Little effort was put into revitalising the accord.

As Aceh's peace deal was being finalized, Sri Lanka's foreign minister was assassinated leading to a state of emergency. Efforts to start high-level talks between the warring parties faltered. On 17 November 2005, Sri Lankans voted in Mahinda Rajapaksa as President who vowed a tough stance against the Tamil fighters. Despite an increase in violence, Rajapaksa's mandate was further endorsed through local election victories in April 2006. More than three more years of brutal fighting ensued before Sri Lanka's government achieved a military victory in mid-2009 with most of the Tamil leaders dead, in combat or by suicide. Rajapaksa was re-elected in January 2010.

Why the difference between the two locations? While Aceh's peace deal was often discussed as having resulted due to the tsunami disaster, Sri Lanka's military solution was not perceived to have been caused by the wave's devastation. Does this situation represent a double standard, in presuming that peace, but not conflict (and see Nelson, 2010a), can be born from disaster? The rebuttal is that the conflict existed anyway, and had existed for decades, so Sri Lanka represented the status quo whilst Aceh appears to be a step change from conflict to peace. Such a statement is overly simplistic on two levels.

First, peace and conflict are not always clear-cut states. The conflicts in both Aceh and Sri Lanka had continued for more than a generation, but so had peace-related efforts, including a string of ceasefires and peace agreements providing occasional respite. Labelling either location through a distinct binary choice of either peace or conflict has not been straightforward throughout the pre-tsunami decades. Even as Aceh moved towards its apparent conflict resolution, it was not obvious that the peace deal would hold in the post-tsunami situation.

Second, correlation is not causation. There is no doubt that the Aceh peace deal was correlated with the tsunami disaster. This correlation does not mean that the Aceh peace deal was caused by the tsunami disaster, especially given the long pre-tsunami history of peace efforts. In Sri Lanka, the subsequent increase in hostilities and the military solution are also correlated with the tsunami disaster. Little basis exists to claim that they were caused by the tsunami disaster given the long pre-tsunami history of the conflict and the wider political forces moving towards hard lines for many of the parties involved.

Moreover, why the difference in outcomes between the two locations? To answer this question, deeper investigation into disaster diplomacy is needed.

2 Introduction

This paper explores the state-of-the-art in 'disaster diplomacy' research and its foreign policy implications. It summarises the current view of disaster diplomacy and some previous case studies which led to this view, while providing new case studies and then interpreting the refined theoretical understanding for policy makers. The importance of this work is in overcoming a standard human and humanitarian assumption that an immediate reaction to a disaster or a prospective disaster is a desire to help and to work together. The reality is that, in political realms, considerations can be prioritised other than providing as much assistance as possible to those in need as soon as possible. The complexities emerging after 26 December 2004 described in section 1 illustrate.

Given these complexities, no assumptions should be made regarding disaster diplomacy, with respect to either its presence or its absence. Instead, when desiring to address conflict, peace, disasters, and their interactions, more theory and evidence are required. Academics and practitioners require a stronger baseline for determining possible pathways, and actions for directing towards or away from certain pathways, when new disaster diplomacy possibilities arise. This paper advances this baseline by providing new case studies feeding into original theoretical analysis. Rather than problematizing disaster diplomacy or its absence—that is, rather than saying that disaster diplomacy or its absence is a problem to be solved—the theory and evidence provided in this paper are about describing disaster diplomacy, understanding how and why it succeeds or fails, and indicating ways forward in which those with influence on disaster diplomacy can make active decisions with regards to foreign policy.

The central argument of this paper is that disaster diplomacy could succeed when those in power decide that they want it to succeed and then use their power for that goal. Despite many media, policy, and humanitarian assumptions that those in power would want and thus would actively seek disaster diplomacy, situations of fully successful disaster diplomacy have not yet been to shown to have occurred, and appear unlikely to occur, because of only disaster-related activities (comprising disaster response and disaster risk reduction). Instead, pre-existing interests towards diplomacy must exist amongst those in power, convincing them that they ought to use their power to achieve disaster diplomacy goals. Such a decision would be made primarily for the pre-existing reasons, not for disaster-related reasons, thereby using disaster diplomacy as an excuse to achieve the diplomatic goals which they wished to achieve anyway.

This argument is demonstrated through bringing together research related to disasters and diplomacy, highlighting the value of inter-disciplinary scholarship through the melding of two fields which have often been distinct. Past work combined with the case studies presented here produce a pattern in which a clear connection is lacking between a disaster and successful diplomacy. In some cases, disasters influenced already existing diplomacy, showing the importance of pre-existing reasons for seeking diplomacy. In other instances, no discernible connection could be evidenced. Consequently, disaster diplomacy is shown to have had limited impact. Consequently, disaster-related activities sometimes catalyse diplomacy in the short-term, but not over the long-term, while disaster-related activities do not create new diplomacy.

The following sections demonstrate the evidence leading to this conclusion and its implications for foreign policy. First, an understanding of the meaning of 'disaster diplomacy' is needed. This understanding is covered in section 3 through theorising disaster and diplomacy, namely by describing theoretical dimensions of each which intersect in disaster diplomacy. Then, section 4 defines and describes disaster diplomacy, providing a framework and research question for presenting two case studies: disease diplomacy in section 5 and climate change diplomacy in section 6. Foreign policy implications emerging from, but going beyond, the case studies are discussed in section 7 in order to lead into section 8 which explains why Sri Lanka and Aceh experienced different diplomacy outcomes following the disaster of 26 December 2004. The final section draws the paper together through an overall conclusion.

This paper does not summarise all the research available nor does it delve deeply into diplomacy or disaster theories, because those topics are extensively covered in the literature already. Instead, the theoretical baseline is the aspects of disaster and diplomacy which meld for disaster diplomacy. Additionally, because implications are discussed for foreign policy, comparatively generic definitions are adopted, rather than the rigid and tight descriptions often sought in academia. Rather than being exclusive to one school of thought on either the disaster or diplomacy sides, this paper seeks to be relevant to an audience incorporating as wide a range of policy makers as feasible, even if it means that some academics might be disappointed at not pinpointing a specific academic theory in either disaster research or diplomacy research.

3 Theorising Disaster and Diplomacy

To investigate and explain disaster diplomacy's foreign policy implications, an understanding of disaster diplomacy is needed. This section provides the needed definitions and integration between the two concepts. Section 3.1 defines the two components of disaster—hazard and vulnerability—followed by explorations of their spatial and temporal overlaps and divergences in Section 3.2. The differing scales segue into section 3.3 detailing the political causes of vulnerability meaning that disaster risk reduction as a political process must be used to address vulnerability, described in section 3.4. This political baseline for vulnerability and hence for disasters connects directly to the importance of diplomacy in the context of disaster-related activities which is covered in section 3.5.

This section builds up a picture demonstrating that disasters are inherently political meaning that diplomacy as a subset of politics has a needed and important role to play in dealing with disasters, through both disaster response and disaster risk reduction and their foreign policy implications. This politics-disaster nexus sets the stage for disaster diplomacy.

3.1 *Hazard and Vulnerability*

A 'disaster' is defined as a situation in which hazard and vulnerability intersect leading to damage or potential damage exceeding the coping capability of those affected without outside support (UNISDR, 2009). The situation's scale could be local, national, or international. The key is that both hazard and vulnerability are required for a disaster to occur.

Hazard refers to a phenomenon, event, or process which has the potential to pose dangers or to cause harm. This definition is general and could refer to almost anything. In a disaster context, hazards are best illustrated by examples.

Hazards emerging from technology which can pose dangers or cause harm include toxic chemicals, electricity, moving parts in machinery, radiation from electronic gear, and vehicles. Aiming to eliminate all hazards would not be viable, because they bring advantages and opportunities alongside their dangers. Instead, some hazards are eliminated, such as banning the pesticide DDT in many countries; some hazards are regulated and controlled, such as laws certifying electrical appliances; and safety measures are legislated, taught, and enforced, such as protective equipment for working in certain sections of nuclear power plants or using robots for access. Hazardousness can be disputed, such as whether or not living near electric power lines causes childhood leukaemia (Draper et al., 2005).

Hazards emerging from the environment which can pose dangers or cause harm include avalanches, blizzards, fog, landslides, lava, and tornadoes. Aiming to eliminate such hazards would not be feasible, because they all bring advantages and opportunities. For example, volcanoes are essential to biogeochemical cycles (James, 2005), floods can fertilise land (Wisner et al., 2004), and seismic faults can make freshwater available in arid locations (Jackson, 2001). Regulating and controlling environmental hazards is tricky, because many are natural processes. Cloud seeding to control precipitation (Bruintjes, 1999) and manipulation of earthquake faults to control earthquakes (Mulargia and Bizzarri, 2014) are attempted, but the results are disputed and are sometimes identified as triggering the hazard which they aimed to control.

Sometimes, social hazards or societal hazards are referred to, not necessarily involving either technology or the environment. Examples are stampedes, riots, terrorism, stock market fluctuations, and bankruptcy potential. Consequent disasters could be fatalities and property damage in stampedes or terrorism; financial crises or recessions occurring following a stock market downturn; and actual bankruptcy or economic problems. These situations start the crossover into defining and understanding vulnerability.

Vulnerability refers to characteristics creating the potential to be harmed (UNISDR, 2009) but also embraces the processes which permit such characteristics to be created and perpetuated in people, infrastructure, communities, and societal systems such as water, energy, and finances (Lewis, 1999; Wisner et al., 2004, 2012). As an example, a building without adequate construction could collapse in an earthquake, hence the lack of adequate construction is the building's vulnerability. Yet knowledge exists to construct buildings to withstand most earthquakes (Coburn and Spence, 2002) meaning that a significant part of the vulnerability is why that knowledge is not applied (Lewis, 2003). The processes which permit a building prone to collapse in an earthquake to be constructed in an earthquake hazard zone are political, covering the lack of building and planning codes alongside the lack of monitoring and enforcement of existing codes. The lack of monitoring and enforcement of existing, adequate building codes was the main reason for the extensive damage experienced in Turkey's earthquake in August 1999 (Spence, 2004)—and in Florida in Hurricane Andrew in August 1992 (Coch, 1995).

Another example of the vulnerability process leading to harm is the 26 December 2004 tsunamis in Aceh and Sri Lanka. As discussed in section 1, the people living in those locations suffered from a long-standing conflict. Locally, the conflicts affected livelihoods, governance, and education, making it difficult for people to have the resources, knowledge, and ability to implement tsunami risk reduction measures. Internationally, the lack of an Indian Ocean tsunami warning system was entirely political through decisions not to allocate resources for it, occurring over the decades after it was first proposed, with full technical know-how available during that time period but not used (Kelman, 2006). These political processes over the long-term represent the vulnerability which meant that most people around the Indian Ocean had neither the knowledge nor the warning to avoid harm from the tsunami. In contrast, the indigenous groups and tourists who had knowledge and who used that knowledge for warning, as described in section 1, had much less vulnerability to tsunamis, so many survived.

The definitions of hazard and vulnerability have ambiguities, as noted for social hazards. Additionally, some of the definitions can be taken to extremes. Gravity is a natural phenomenon which could be said to 'cause' slides such as avalanches, landslides, and rockfalls, but gravity is essential for life. Should the hazard be termed 'gravity' or 'slides'? Is the 'disaster' of a fall from a height caused by the hazard of gravity; the vulnerability of people to impacting the ground after falling; or the vulnerability of people and social systems in failing to prevent the fall?

These questions are more about philosophy and parsing than they are about disaster-related activities. Without denying their relevance (for example, Wyss and Peppoloni, 2015), the text here does not address them, instead accepting the definitions given as being suitable for many pragmatic purposes, including the analysis of disaster diplomacy and its foreign policy implications. Similarly, many theories use different constructs for vulnerability, incorporating vocabulary such as 'exposure', 'susceptibility', and 'resilience'. Here, those components are accepted as being encompassed by the vulnerability process in order to retain a straightforward understanding of disaster as requiring the intersection of hazard and vulnerability.

Hazard and vulnerability themselves are not entirely independent. The presence, layout, and shape of buildings affects flood parameters such as depth and velocity. Fog alone does not affect vehicles, but the choice to drive or to fly in fog, without adjusting one's behaviour for the fog, sets up the potential for collisions. The existence of vulnerability can determine how hazardous a regular environmental phenomenon becomes. On 22 December 2003, an earthquake of magnitude 6.5 at 8 km depth shook central California. Two people died when a clock tower collapsed. For most people experiencing this tremor, it had little impact on them. Four days later, a similar earthquake, of magnitude 6.6 at 10 km (so slightly stronger and slightly deeper) hit southeast Iran killing over 25,000 people, particularly in the city of Bam where many were killed when adobe dwellings collapsed, despite knowledge existing about making adobe dwellings safe in earthquakes (Blondet et al., 2003). Many other parameters dictate the shaking experiencing by a building during an earthquake, including rock and soil type between the building and the wave origins; distance from the wave origins; foundation design and construction; and engineering and landscaping around the building.

In December 2003, the large difference in death toll was almost exclusively due to vulnerability, including population numbers; population and building density; and building materials and construction practices. In California, vulnerability was low, so the earthquake as a hazard was highly localised to a single building failure which killed two people. In Iran, vulnerability was high, so the earthquake was a major hazard and the intersection of hazard and vulnerability led to a disaster. Vulnerability rather than hazard is the main determinant of disaster consequences.

3.2 *Disaster Scales*

The lesson of vulnerability causing disasters applies to disasters across all time and space scales. This lesson is also reinforced by examining disasters at different scales.

Some definitions of 'disaster' assign quantitative measures. The International Disaster Database (EM-DAT, 2015) in Belgium adds a disaster to their database only if (i) fatalities are ten or more; or (ii) a hundred or more people are affected; or (iii) there is a declaration of a state of emergency; or (iv) there is a call for international assistance. Neither the hazard's type nor its characteristics are part of this definition. Instead, as one strength of EM-DAT's approach, the focus is on impacts, highlighting the vulnerability necessary for a disaster to occur.

Desinventar (2015) is another disaster database and takes a similar approach, focusing on impacts in order to emphasise vulnerability. This database does not define 'disaster', instead recording 'events' which are often hazards and then detailing the impacts of those hazards (OSSO and La Red, 2009). Consequently, it captures effects at all scales without an arbitrary cut-off. If hail smashes roofs and crushes crops in a village of 80 people without fatalities, then it would be calamitous for that village yet no criterion for EM-DAT would be met. Desinventar would recognise the situation as a disaster and would include it in its database.

Certainly, the larger the spatial scale and the more compressed the time scale, the more attention a disaster tends to garner. That is, the larger the area or the number of people affected and the shorter the time over which these effects manifest, the more prominent a disaster tends to be. Prominence does not necessarily correlate with overall impacts. Analysis of Desinventar's data for Colombia indicates that accumulated effects of smaller disasters are far greater than those of large disasters (Marulanda et al., 2010).

This empirical analysis matches with earlier theory (La Red et al., 2002; Lewis, 1984) that most disasters are local and are experienced locally, even if a hazard is large-scale. A community's vulnerability and disaster impacts are not always seen beyond the affected communities. Disasters hitting international headlines, generating external humanitarian responses, and potentially influencing or being influenced by foreign policy tend to be exceptions. Instead, vulnerability dictates that small-scale events lead to small-scale impacts which accumulate and prevent people from improving their livelihoods and living conditions over the long-term (in the absence of development-related interventions, which could come from inside the community, outside, or both). These small-scale disasters are termed 'invisible' (La Red et al., 2002), occurring due to accrued 'invisible vulnerability' which typically manifests or is recognised only when a hazard appears.

As such, vulnerability impacts disaster far more than hazard by creating conditions in which a disaster can be realised with any hazard from a wide array. Vulnerability is a regular, chronic process, lived by people day-to-day due to the political (including diplomatic and foreign policy related) and social circumstances in which they find themselves (Lewis, 1999; Wisner et al., 2004, 2012). Certain hazards may be exceptional, extreme, rare, and hard to predict. Disasters cannot be described by any of these, or related, adjectives because the vulnerability is ever-present, known, and typical. The vulnerability process causes the disaster, even if the vulnerability process is revealed and noted only after a disaster has occurred in the context of a specific hazard.

The time scale of a disaster is thus long-term because the vulnerability process takes place over long times scales. A hazard can appear suddenly, such as an earthquake in seconds or a flash flood in minutes. Even the hours or days of warning afforded by many storms and non-flash floods are rarely enough time to undo the years and decades of prior vulnerability accrual. Consequently, a hazard might be sudden-onset (appearing over short time scales, such as earthquakes) or slow-onset (appearing over long time scales, such as droughts). Irrespective of the hazard's time scale, the disaster is inevitably slow-onset (appearing over long time scales) since the vulnerability process requires long time scales to reach the state at which a disaster occurs.

Following an earthquake disaster, Los Angeles promulgated its first seismic-related building code in 1933 (Levy and Salvadori, 1995) leading to a long history of Californian efforts to improve structural earthquake safety. Each earthquake brought new lessons. Most Californian earthquake designs had considered mainly horizontal shaking until the Northridge earthquake of 1994 caused most damage from vertical shaking, leading to building code revisions (Coch, 1995). The successive lessons, often following fatalities and gleaned over decades, contributed to the low death toll in the 2003 earthquake.

The situation in Bam, Iran had similarly developed over a long time period. The city's heritage dates back millennia, as recognised in its classification as a UNESCO World Heritage Site. The governance conditions in Iran causing the lack of earthquake-resistant design, despite the knowledge being available and promoted by Iranian scientists (Nateghi-A, 1997), are enmeshed in politics over decades, including American and British foreign policy, continuing post-colonial legacies, dictatorship, oppression, and resource allocation. Neither California's nor Iran's situation in 2003 was caused quickly or by the respective earthquakes. Instead, the vulnerability process over the long-term led to the conditions which were exposed in vastly different outcomes by similar tremors just four days apart.

Given the disconnect in scales between hazard and vulnerability, and that hazard parameters do not have as much impact on a disaster as the vulnerability process, a tenet from disaster theory is that 'natural disasters' is an inadequate phrase, effectively being a misnomer. Because disaster is not caused by a hazard, even if an environmentally-related hazard such as a flood or a volcanic eruption is involved, the disaster cannot be considered to be natural or environmental. Because vulnerability is a regular situation experienced day-to-day by many in the populace, disasters are not a natural state of affairs, instead being the norm, expected, and unexceptional (see also Hewitt, 1983).

This ethos applies to technological hazards and to social hazards, also sometimes indicating the blurring between hazard and vulnerability. Perrow's (1998) theory of 'normal accidents' indicates that, for technological systems, 'accidents' are typical, expected, and continual because of the systems creating these conditions—exactly like the vulnerability process.

The lessons from exploring disaster scales are apparent. First, without denigrating the large-scale catastrophes, the small-scale ones which rarely reach the news or the scientific literature have immense impact due to vulnerability, irrespective of the hazards involved. Second, vulnerability emerges from long-term, wide-scale social impetuses, even if the effects manifest locally when a short-term hazard manifests.

3.3 *Political Causes of Vulnerability*

Vulnerability arises from many factors, rooted in long-term societal processes which build and retain characteristics leading to the potential to be harmed. This analysis demonstrates that vulnerability is fundamentally political.

Few people want or expect to die in disasters, yet it frequently occurs. Some people make choices which augment their vulnerability, such as purchasing expensive beachfront properties in Hilton Head, South Carolina or Barbados and then deciding not to evacuate when a hurricane warning is issued. Others do not have the resources to make choices regarding where and how they live such as in the informal settlements of Manila or Los Angeles.

Sometimes, the lack of choices in dealing with hazards emerges at an individual, day-to-day level. Poor people tend to die more frequently in temperature extremes in large cities because in hot weather they cannot afford the electricity cost of air conditioning or fans (Klinenberg, 2002) and in cold weather they cannot afford the cost of heating (Rudge and Gilchrist, 2005). For storms, without funds or friends/family to support alternative accommodation or public transportation to public disaster shelters, evacuating in the face of storm warnings is not an easy choice for poorer people. In Bangladesh, some families refused to evacuate following a cyclone warning because they did not wish to abandon their livestock which was their main livelihood source; providing for livestock protection and care during the cyclone encouraged many to go to shelters (Cash et al., 2013).

Sometimes, the lack of choices in dealing with hazards is more due to social structures, at the societal level. Neumayer and Plümper (2007) demonstrate how physical differences between males and females cannot explain differential mortality in disasters involving different types of hazards across 141 countries from 1981–2002. Instead, they highlight socioeconomic status and other gender-based roles which society imposes on males and females as creating or reducing vulnerability in disasters. These factors are social and political, not biological, making disasters and vulnerability gendered (Enarson and Morrow, 1998). Highlighting individual gender characteristics as causing vulnerability, or claiming that females are inherently or naturally more vulnerable than males in disasters, neglects the societally constructed causes of gender-differentiated vulnerability.

Therefore, vulnerability is fundamentally political, meaning that disasters (emerging from vulnerability) are fundamentally political, rather than being natural or environmental. Vulnerability is created and maintained through societal choice, deliberate or inadvertent. The usual circumstances are that certain groups who have more choices and power foist vulnerability on other groups who have fewer choices and less power, such as men imposing gender roles on men and women, creating vulnerability for both.

Voluntary shifts of power to give people choices about their own vulnerabilities do not always occur, meaning that communities might decide they must take power. Violent conflict is one possible result. Alternatively, external interventions might assist, such as for disaster risk reduction, with those interventions potentially being part of foreign policy and thus involving diplomacy.

Researchers can also act as catalysts to break down barriers amongst community groups and to break through exclusion of some of the groups. An example is work in the Philippines using collaborative community hazard and vulnerability analysis to bring together minority and majority groups for reducing vulnerability to landslides, road crashes, droughts, and floods

(Gaillard et al., 2011). At other times, change might need to be imposed. The National Flood Insurance Program in the U.S.A. illustrates a top-down national initiative aimed at flood risk reduction (Kunreuther and White, 1994). In these cases, the technical measures are usually straightforward, but getting them implemented, monitored, and enforced entails carefully working through the social, power-related, and political structures and norms—that is, tackling vulnerability.

3.4 *Addressing Political Causes Through Disaster Risk Reduction*

Overcoming the political and power challenges in order to achieve vulnerability reduction is the baseline for disaster risk reduction, although it is not the only activity. Disaster risk reduction refers to policies and actions targeting the root causes of disasters so that actual and potential damage are reduced (UNISDR, 2009). Actions focus on reducing vulnerability, such as by giving boys and girls equal access to education and ensuring that a variety of community voices is heard regarding livelihoods initiatives. Disaster risk reduction can include tackling hazards directly, such as by erecting walls outside a town to deflect avalanches. Endeavours might bring together hazards and vulnerabilities through a community analysing hazards and selecting its own planning process for retrofits and new developments such that vulnerability is reduced.

At the international policy level, the Sendai Framework for Disaster Risk Reduction (UNISDR, 2015) is a voluntary agreement coordinated by the UN Office for Disaster Risk Reduction (UNISDR) and running from 2015–2030. The Sendai Framework succeeds the Hyogo Framework for Action (UNISDR, 2005) which was also voluntary and coordinated by UNISDR.

Because the UNISDR initiatives are voluntary, many countries adopt national legislative approaches for disaster risk reduction. Following the replacement of apartheid with full parliamentary democracy, South Africa shifted from a militaristic culture of civil defence to disaster risk reduction, embodied in a green paper leading to a white paper inputting into the Disaster Management Act of 2002 (Vermaak and van Niekerk, 2004). It is lauded as good practice in national disaster risk reduction legislation despite not mentioning ethnicity (Wisner et al., 2004) and despite its apparent failure in tackling HIV/AIDS, crime, and road crashes. Mongolia's 2003 Law on Disaster Protection is similarly highlighted as a model for other countries to emulate (Jeggle, 2013), but many vulnerability challenges remain and the country remains low in numerous development indicators (HDR, 2014). The situations in South Africa and Mongolia do not indicate that national legislation is unnecessary, merely that it is insufficient on its own. The U.S.A. has had national disaster relief legislation since 1974 and the Disaster Mitigation Act was passed in 2000, but the national legislation and the country's vast disaster risk reduction and disaster response experience did not stop foreseeable and devastating failures at national, state, and local levels for Hurricane Katrina in 2005, including the abject failure of disaster diplomacy when the national government seemed neither ready for nor interested in international assistance (Kelman, 2007).

Beyond top-down legislative and voluntary measures, disaster risk reduction is frequently conducted through bottom-up initiatives while recognising that all approaches have advantages and limitation; there is no ideal (Aldrich, 2012; Twigg, 1999–2000). Local teams focusing on disaster response, but demonstrating their contributions to disaster risk reduction, exist around the world, from Taiwan (Chen et al., 2006) to Haiti (Carlile et al., 2014). Tasks of community-based teams can range from identifying water and gas pipelines and their shutoff points (disaster response) which helps to monitor for sections requiring maintenance (disaster risk reduction), through to identifying people living alone who might need extra post-disaster help (disaster response), which helps to better connect community members (disaster risk reduction).

In conducting an assessment of likely infrastructure failures, rescue needs, and subsequent training, a physical vulnerability analysis is necessarily completed, suggesting possibilities for reducing this vulnerability. In conducting an assessment of community members, their capabilities, and their likely post-disaster needs, a social vulnerability analysis is necessarily completed, suggesting possibilities for reducing this vulnerability. Disaster response and disaster risk reduction are intricately linked, supporting each other.

All these processes are political far more than they are technical. They involve cultural norms (IFRC, 2014; Krüger et al., 2015), power relations (Krüger et al., 2015; Wisner et al., 2004, 2012), and inequalities (Hewitt, 1983; Wisner et al., 2004, 2012). The overarching approach for disaster risk reduction tends to be tackling these root causes of vulnerability which deny large swathes of the population opportunities to reduce their own vulnerability. Rather than using force, imposition, and takeovers to achieve these ends, doing so requires cautious, deft politicking plus the navigation human relations; that is, politics, both domestic and international. Diplomatic processes become key to achieving effective disaster risk reduction and disaster response.

3.5 *Theorising Diplomacy in the Context of Disaster-related Activities*

The previous sections theorised disaster, indicating that disasters are political (which involves diplomacy) in that the fundamental cause of disasters is people and institutions with different interests and resources jockeying to promote those interests and resources—including through foreign policy. This section uses this basis to theorise diplomacy in the context of disaster-related activities (disaster response and disaster risk reduction) in order to provide background for understanding and exploring disaster diplomacy. Fundamentally, power and political games produce vulnerability, usually with one sector of the population producing vulnerability in another sector. One subset of politics and power games is the interactions of governments. These interactions can be conducted peacefully, neutrally, or hostilely, with the latter including violent and non-violent conflict.

The peaceful interaction of governments and government entities has been proposed as one baseline definition for 'diplomacy' (Bull, 1977). Many other baseline definitions have been provided, such as Nicolson's (1939) focus on official representatives of governments negotiating peacefully in the context of international relations, although he generalises later to refer to diplomacy as different groups interacting in an ordered manner. Nicolson (1939) further sought a clear and specific definition for 'diplomacy', but that is hard to achieve in reality, as shown by the development of theories of diplomacy and how they are put into policy and practice.

In particular, further words from the baseline definitions need to be defined and clarified. For example, what are the meanings of 'peacefully', 'official', and even 'government'? Gunboat diplomacy (Cable, 1971) is about using military threats from a navy (easily expanded to other military forces) to achieve foreign policy objectives. It is ostensibly peaceful and diplomatic (soft power, as per Nye, 1990), yet pointedly carries the threat of violence and coercion (hard power).

Meanwhile, with the growth of influence on foreign affairs of non-state entities, the labels 'official' and 'government' have become nebulous. As noted in section 1, ensuring that humanitarian aid reached populations in need in Aceh and Sri Lanka meant negotiating with non-governmental groups. In situations where more than one group claims to be the government, or where not all states recognise a government—with diverse, contemporary examples being North Cyprus, Sahrawi Arab Democratic Republic, and Somalia/Somaliland—negotiations might be needed with different parties, irrespective of their 'official' or 'governmental' level.

Beyond the definitional discussions, the reality of diplomacy has moved away from trained and accredited diplomats being the sole proprietors of foreign policy and international politics. For some disasters, such as landmines and HIV/AIDS, 'celebrity diplomacy' has gained prominence with mixed effectiveness (Cooper, 2008). The media have frequently been implicated in disaster-related foreign policy endeavours, from goading and inhibiting wars (Kamalipour and Snow, 2004) to galvanising post-disaster foreign aid. During the Mozambique floods of 2000, video of a woman giving birth in a tree, amongst other dramatic helicopter rescues, significantly augmented the international aid response (Olsen et al., 2003).

This reality of who does diplomacy is reflected in the literature through analyses of diplomacy 'tracks'. Two tracks of diplomacy were defined by Davidson and Montville (1981). Track One diplomacy covers diplomacy according to Nicolson (1939) and Bull (1977); in effect, official governmental diplomacy conducted by civil servants, diplomats, and politicians. Track Two diplomacy is explicitly about unofficial, potentially unstructured, and not necessarily governmental interactions. Scientists, celebrities, and cultural and sports exchanges sit within it. The two-track diplomacy framework was expanded by Diamond and McDonald (1993) to 'multi-track diplomacy' through nine separate tracks: 1. Government; 2. Professional conflict resolution; 3. Business; 4. Private citizens; 5. Research, training and education; 6. Activism; 7. Religious; 8. Funding; and 9. Public opinion/communication.

The nine tracks divide institutions such as government and business from purposes such as funding and activism, even though a single institution might embrace many of these purposes. Institutions not listed include international organisations, both intergovernmental and non-governmental, and the media. As well, the tracks are not mutually exclusive or conducted alone. Businesses can negotiate with governments and other businesses in another country. Private citizens, celebrities or not, can be involved in activism, research, and funding. In their work, Diamond and McDonald (1993) deal with some dimensions of these points. Notably, the expansion of diplomacy into multiple tracks, with overlaps and connections amongst the tracks, pushes diplomacy beyond the strict realm of interactions amongst different sovereign states. As noted above, governments might not exist, might not be viable as negotiating entities, or might not be fully recognised.

Diplomacy in research, policy, and practice has evolved further. State diplomats cannot represent their country's interests by compartmentalising their activities into neatly separated tracks. Many specialise in specific themes such as environment or security. A need still exists to work across and to bring together sectors while maintaining a level of generalisation in order to connect different fields and topics—even while being supported by technical specialists who might be experts in a geographic region such as southeast Asia or in a topic such as biodiversity. Kurbalija and Katrandjiev's (2006) description and analysis of multi-stakeholder diplomacy provides the varied techniques and creative approaches characterising modern diplomacy.

It is not just the parties involved and the networks developed to effect diplomacy, but also the negotiating spaces and information flows created. Section 6 details climate change diplomacy for which one anecdote repeated from the 2015 UN climate negotiations was the apparent use of a Zulu and Xhosa technique, indaba, to move forward the agreement's draft text. Meanwhile, Fisher (2013) and Zaharna et al. (2014) describe the importance of information flows for public diplomacy, highlighting pathways such as social media and migrants. As in many other instances, diplomats cannot cast themselves as authority figures from whom the public will take and apply sage advice. Instead, public diplomacy is a multi-level conversation in which diplomats listen and learn as well as providing and teaching. Consequently, creating networks and interaction spaces for those networks becomes a key element of diplomacy, including but not limited to the national level.

With supranational entities such as the European Union being involved in formal and informal diplomacy—and even having separate membership status in international organisations such as the United Nations Framework Convention on Climate Change—the diplomatic power of sovereign states is being pooled in some cases. Meanwhile, the rise of para-diplomacy—which is particularly evident for island jurisdictions (Baldacchino and Milne, 2009) but with other notable examples being Québec, Scotland, and Catalonia—has diluted state power for many diplomatic endeavours. Para-diplomacy has been enacted for disaster-related activities, both disaster risk reduction and disaster response (Kelman et al., 2006).

Many international institutions involved in disaster-related activities, both before and after a disaster, do not shy away from interactions at the national, supranational, and subnational levels (Hollis, 2015) or using diplomacy in different ways and forms. Within disaster response, humanitarian diplomacy is one process, in effect being the use of diplomacy to achieve humanitarian aims (Acuto, 2014; Minear and Smith, 2007). The International Federation of Red Cross and Red Crescent Societies openly and actively uses humanitarian diplomacy to achieve its organisational aims (IFRC, 2009).

The UN's disaster-related focal points are UNISDR for disaster risk reduction and the Office for the Coordination of Humanitarian Affairs (UNOCHA) for disaster response. Regional supranational organisations for disaster-related activities include the EU's Humanitarian Aid and Civil Protection department (ECHO), the Secretariat of the Pacific Community's Applied Geoscience and Technology Division (SPC SOPAC), and the Caribbean Disaster Emergency Management Agency (CDEMA). The Caribbean and the Pacific regions separate climate change from disaster-related activities and have different supranational organisations dealing with climate change.

ECHO works within the EU's legal framework, such as responding when member states request assistance and balancing with EU and national legislation. ECHO also implements subsidiarity as an EU principle, working with governments in the context of other transboundary collaborations, such as for the Arctic through The Northern Dimension which involves the EU, Russia, Norway and Iceland. In the Caribbean and the Pacific regions, the regional agencies work directly with national governments, subnational authorities, and communities for disaster-related activities. Because many of the island countries are small, they recognise that their governments do not always have the capacity or resources for disaster-related activities. They pool their resources and expertise in the regional agencies which then gather international donor support, in funds and in personnel, to work in the member countries at all governance levels.

All these intergovernmental interactions and networks at different levels comprise diplomacy—yet clearly do not cover all intergovernmental or inter-state interactions and networks. Consequently, diplomacy sits as one subset of intergovernmental and inter-state interactions focusing on peaceful interactions and information exchanges. Intergovernmental and interstate interactions are themselves one subset of politics, placing diplomacy as one subset within the wide realm of politics.

Overlaps are also seen with respect to the individuals involved. By definition, the role of diplomats is to do diplomacy while the role of politicians is to do politics. With diplomacy as a subset of politics, the roles are not entirely divorced, irrespective of individual diplomatic and political roles being held by the same or different individuals. Many diplomats never enter politics whilst many politicians rarely do diplomacy. Some politicians take diplomatic jobs, such as ex-ministers being appointed to ambassadorial roles or the ex-Prime Minister of New Zealand, Helen Clark, becoming the Administrator of the United Nations Development Programme (UNDP). The American President Barack Obama had two Secretaries of State, Hillary Clinton and John Kerry, both of whom were appointed from the position of being an elected Senator. How each individual transitions from and to different roles vary. Some switch decisively while others bring their previous job's personality to their new role, with differing levels of success and failure. Mary Robinson, formerly Ireland's elected President which is a ceremonial role, ended her post as the United Nations High Commissioner for Human Rights by indicating that she felt unable to do her work. Her statement could be seen to represent her failure to do the job well or her success in terms of ruffling diplomatic feathers through her dedication to human rights principles.

While the theorisation of diplomacy in the context of disaster-related activities in today's world might not give a strong definition or delineation according to Nicolson's (1939) ethos, it is in line with a pragmatic perspective of theories describing how diplomacy happens today with all its complexities. This discussion provides an understanding (not definition) of the meanings of diplomacy for disaster-related activities, so that 'disaster diplomacy' can now be defined and elucidated.

4 Theorising Disaster Diplomacy

With the understanding of disaster and diplomacy, and their connections, from section 3, the two concepts can now be combined to explain and understand disaster diplomacy, as is completed in this section. A wide swathe of literature exists surrounding the disaster-politics nexus (De Boer and Sanders, 2004, 2005; Glantz, 1976; Hewitt, 1983; Lewis, 1999; Olson and Drury, 1997; Drury and Olson, 1998; Wisner et al., 2004). As is clear from the vulnerability theory in section 3, disasters, disaster risk reduction, and disaster response by definition are political, one dimension of which is about diplomacy. As with humanitarian diplomacy using diplomacy to achieve humanitarian aims, diplomacy can be used as a mechanism to achieve disaster risk reduction in addition to disaster response.

Does or could the reverse occur? Could disasters achieve or cause diplomacy? Disaster diplomacy is a field of research investigating this question, including related policy and practice questions. Expanded in this section, disaster diplomacy investigates how and why disaster-related activities do and do not influence conflict and cooperation.

Section 4.1 summarises past examples which are considered to represent disaster diplomacy. The conclusion from much of the past theoretical and case study literature is that disaster diplomacy tends not to be observed—that is, disasters do not cause or create diplomacy—yet section 4.2 explains how poignant critiques emerge that this work does not fully draw on history nor does it provide clear definitions. Thus, it is important to ask and answer the question: 'What is success?' for disaster diplomacy? To assist in answering this question, section 4.3. introduces two theoretical notions to apply to the case studies: Intentionality and foreseeability. The application of these notions leads to section 4.4 examining ethical implications which result.

In setting up and defining disaster diplomacy, this section covers background to previous literature, debates, and gaps, indicating how theory and case studies build on each other to paint a fuller picture of disaster diplomacy. A basis is provided for considering how further examples could assist in explaining the foreign policy implications of disaster diplomacy.

4.1 *Previous Disaster Diplomacy Examples*

Numerous disaster diplomacy case studies have been published, both individually and as meta-analyses, reaching far back into history. A sampling of vignettes is provided here, not providing a full literature review, but instead summarising while indicating some of the foreign policy implications.

Nel and Righarts (2008) discuss an earthquake striking Sparta in 465/464 BC which is attributed to being the trigger of a slave revolt. Being a trigger is different from being a cause and no intimation is made that the slave-Spartan conflict was caused by an earthquake, since slavery itself is cause enough for an uprising. In fact, Urbainczyk (2008) documents numerous slave rebellions in Sparta noting that the slaves 'took advantage of… the chaos caused by an earthquake' (p. 24) in 464 BC to escape and to live freely, only to be attacked by the Spartans seeking to bring them back into slavery. Several of the rebellions occurred during wars, with the slaves taking advantage of the ongoing conflict to generate further conflict which might free them. The earthquake and wars provided opportunities to seek freedom rather than being the cause of the revolutions.

Some of the case studies demonstrate the complexities of understanding disaster diplomacy related decisions. Segalla (2012) researches the American government's response to 10,000 people being paralysed in Morocco in 1959 due to contaminated cooking oil. The contamination occurred when Moroccan merchants purchased engine oil from a US Air Force base in the country, adding it to cooking oil to increase their profit margin. The paralysis occurred because the engine oil was contaminated with a poison which might not have been legal in Morocco. Already, unravelling responsibility for the situation becomes difficult. The American government was careful regarding acknowledging culpability and providing aid. The provision of aid for the poisoning disaster was further complicated by floods occurring beforehand and an earthquake occurring afterwards, for which American aid to Moroccans was used as part of Cold War related public diplomacy. Segalla (2012) concludes that in each instance, and considering the combined effect of all disasters, post-disaster aid from the Americans became a political tool, seeking to garner support from Morocco for the American presence. Ultimately, it did not work and the Americans closed their base in 1963, as had been previously agreed.

Olson and Drury (1997) and Drury and Olson (1998) analysed conflict-disaster connections for case studies from 1966–1980. Worse disasters tended to ferment political violence while political repressiveness decreased post-disaster political problems. For the former point, people would take advantage of the disaster situation to push forward political agendas, an opportunity quashed by heavy-handed governments leading to the latter point. Lewis (1999) explored case studies in the 1970s, considering how a cyclone affected East Pakistan in 1970 and how an earthquake affected Nicaragua in 1972. Each situation contributed significantly to brewing political conflicts. A separatist war in East Pakistan soon led to the founding of Bangladesh while Nicaragua's dictator fled the country in 1979 when rebels marched into the capital city and took over.

In neither case, did the disaster cause the conflict, but it did provide a major spark amongst other influencing factors. Even more importantly, Lewis' (1999) discussion indicates that it was not the disaster per se which catalysed each conflict, but each government's inadequate response to the disaster. Aid was mismanaged and, particularly in Nicaragua, blatant corruption incensed the population, turning them even further away from the government (see also De Boer and Sanders, 2005; Olson, 2000). Each disaster, perhaps, could have been an opportunity for the respective governments to win back support from the population by helping the people, but the governments failed to grasp the opportunities.

In terms of disasters potentially leading to conflict resolution, many contemporary examples have been thoroughly researched. As summarised from Ker-Lindsay (2000, 2007), a remarkable turnaround occurred in Greek-Turkish relations following two earthquakes in 1999. On 17 August 1999, approximately 17,000 people were killed by a tremor in Turkey. Within 30 minutes, Athens and Ankara were making high-level contact and Turkey accepted extensive Greek assistance. The aid was not confined to the governments. Greeks, their religious institutions, their media, and their community groups offered support, empathy, donations, and assistance.

Three weeks later, the solidarity with Turkey and the positive media coverage of Turks in need, with Greece having a responsibility to help, had not diminished. Nonetheless, some dissenting voices were starting to be heard above the supportive clamour. On 7 September 1999, more than 100 people died when an earthquake shook Athens. In response, Turkey reciprocated what Greece had previously provided. The Turkish government, media, religious groups, and communities did exactly as the Greeks had done in offering assistance. The Greeks did as the Turks did, graciously accepting the offers. Soon, Greece was actively supporting Turkey entering the European Union and commentators were extolling a new era of 'earthquake diplomacy'. The media were particularly prominent in giving coverage to the aid responses while proclaiming a new era of Greek-Turkish cooperation.

Ker-Lindsay (2000, 2007) burst the bubble of the earthquakes creating the diplomacy, showing that the rapprochement went back to April 1999, when the Kosovo conflict threatened to destabilise the Balkans. Greece and Turkey had started quiet diplomacy behind the scenes to avert spillover of and from the war. These connections, including the personal friendship of the two foreign ministers, had provided a foundation for the post-earthquake diplomacy.

Mavrogenis and Kelman (2013) trace the process back earlier, to 1996 when political élites in the two countries decided that looking to the future meant looking to reconciliation (see also Ker-Lindsay, 2007). The seeds of Greece and Turkey coming together had been planted then, were reinforced over the Kosovo conflict, and—as Ker-Lindsay (2000, 2007) describes—were exposed to the public spotlight after the earthquakes. This exposure gave the people of both countries something tangible to grasp and almost destroyed the process by giving detractors clear targets. Because of the years of careful work on both sides, not because of the earthquakes, the process lasted, surviving changes in government on both sides; further earthquakes, floods, and storms; the Eurocrisis alongside Turkey's democracy crisis; terrorism in Turkey; and the war in Syria accompanied by a major refugee influx into Europe. Perhaps each country simply has much more to worry about than each other, but politically at the moment, it is hard to label the two countries as enemies. The 1999 earthquakes were one input amongst many towards Greece-Turkey diplomacy, but the earthquake diplomacy surged forward based on pre-earthquake politics.

A similarly incisive analysis was provided by Holloway's (2000) description of the 1991–1993 drought emergency across southern Africa. The drought emergency did not turn into a drought disaster because the affected countries cooperated to import food despite vicious past conflicts which were just in the end phase. Holloway (2000) concluded that the state of diplomacy dictated the aid response, not that drought diplomacy occurred. A major catastrophe was averted because the countries of the region worked together and overcame the remnants of the violent conflicts to succeed in a massive food import. They collaborated on the humanitarian operation not because of the drought, but because they were collaborating anyway to transition to a post-apartheid South Africa and a post-conflict Southern Africa.

Soon after Fidel Castro seized power in Havana in 1959, Cuba and the U.S.A. ended up at loggerheads. As Glantz (2000) writes, parties on both sides worked hard to ensure that no disaster would change this adversarial situation. Part of Castro's ability to retain power as a dictator rested on having a big enemy which he would stand up against. The U.S.A. provided that enemy. The American government, initially hurting from Castro having removed the Americans' own dictator/ally and then being subservient to the powerful Cuban exile lobby which opposed any politician who dared suggest reconciliation with Castro, found itself locked into isolating Cuba. Part of the isolation was the American government imposing a trade embargo on Cuba. Despite numerous disasters affecting Cuba, American aid was sporadic. When possibilities were found to circumvent the trade embargo for disaster aid, such as during a 1998 drought, Fidel Castro creatively found excuses to avoid accepting American aid, often blaming the trade embargo for Cuba's need for post-disaster assistance. The lack of disaster diplomacy worked both ways. After Hurricane Katrina in 2005, Cuba offered aid to the U.S.A. which was refused (noting that refusing aid is not uncommon; Nelson, 2010b).

In 2006, Fidel's brother Raúl Castro assumed Cuba's presidency, first in an acting capacity and then with full power in 2008. He implemented numerous changes, including a thawing towards the U.S.A. The small, careful steps which all happened in the absence of significant disaster-related influences led to the restoration of Cuba-U.S.A. diplomatic relations in 2015. The change in situation was due to the change in Cuban leadership rather than due to disaster-related activities.

As Cuba moved closer to the U.S.A., Iran moved farther away. Warnaar's (2013) title sums up the situation: American-Iranian relations were 'Shaken, Not Stirred' by disaster, in this instance the 26 December 2003 earthquake in Iran which killed over 25,000 people. Earlier earthquakes in Iran, such as in 1990 and 2002, had led to a small amount of American aid arriving, but without marked impact on diplomacy. 2003 appeared to be different. The U.S.A. offered aid which Iran accepted, seemingly resulting in a political thawing between the two countries which spurred on extensive media speculation of earthquake diplomacy. Kelman (2012) traced this apparent thawing back several months to ongoing reconciliation attempts in conjunction with wider geopolitical efforts in the region aiming to bring Iran closer to other countries to which it was hostile. One such country was Egypt which also provided earthquake aid. Israel is an exception. Iran made it clear that Israeli aid would not be accepted after the earthquake.

Over the weeks immediately following the 2003 earthquake, little diplomatic progress was made. Iran stipulated that the aid was for humanitarian, not political, reasons and rebuffed American attempts to push forward the diplomacy. By the end of January 2004, with earthquake recovery barely started, disaster diplomacy hopes had faded. 2004 was a major election year in both countries, with those in power in each country needing to portray the other as an enemy in order to gain votes. Another earthquake hit southern Iran on 22 February 2005 killing over 600 people, leading to an American offer of aid which was declined. Just over six months later, Iran's offer to assist the U.S.A. following Hurricane Katrina was declined.

In the decade since then, Iran's relations with the U.S.A. and other countries in the region has remained hostile with difficult negotiations over Iran's nuclear programmes and with tension over American involvement in Iraq and Afghanistan. One of the major advances in Iran-U.S.A. diplomacy occurred in mid-2015 with the signing of a deal between Iran and China, France, Germany, Russia, the U.K., and the U.S.A. In exchange for Iran giving concessions on its nuclear activity, sanctions would be lifted. Whether or not the agreement is ratified and implemented, it represents a major breakthrough after nearly two years of tortuous negotiations representing the power of diplomacy (Bohlen, 2015)—without much influence from disaster-related activities.

This pattern is repeated by India and Pakistan. From the moment that both countries achieved independence in August 1947, they were in political and military conflict with each other, including a race for nuclear weapons. Disasters affecting each country, and sometimes both together, had little impact on the state of affairs, even after cooperation incidences such as in May 1999 when Pakistani authorities rescued Indian fishermen from Gujarat following a storm.

Then, on 26 January 2001, an earthquake shook western India, killing more than 20,000 people. Almost immediately, Pakistan offered assistance which led to a summit of India's and Pakistan's leaders from 14–16 July 2001. Despite, or because of, high hopes and intense scrutiny for the earthquake to create peace between the two countries, a final statement on the summit to be signed by both leaders could not be agreed. In the ensuing months, the two leaders exchanged insults and accusations. Compounded with terrorist attacks in each country which were blamed on the other side, the world feared the prospect of a nuclear war.

On 8 October 2005, hopes for earthquake diplomacy were revived after more than 70,000 people were killed in an earthquake disaster in the Kashmir region, parts of which have disputed claims by China, India, and Pakistan. The de facto India-Pakistan border in Kashmir, the 'Line of Control', was opened briefly to permit people and supplies to cross, but little change beyond prior India-Pakistan reconciliation initiatives was seen. A cross-border bus service had already started earlier that year, so efforts to ease post-earthquake cross-border restrictions were an extension of previous initiatives. Meanwhile, political disagreements hampered the use of Indian helicopters in Pakistan for rescue and relief.

Both countries seemed to be tiptoeing around earthquake diplomacy, conscious that they wished to continue the slow diplomacy they had developed over the previous few years while providing earthquake relief, but without repeating the 2001 debacle. The strategy seems to have succeeded. The response to the Kashmir earthquake proceeded, albeit slowly. India-Pakistan rapprochement has continued despite changes in governments, further disasters, multiple terrorist attacks, and continuing flashpoints in the region including Afghanistan and Nepal.

The commonalities amongst these case studies, and many others (Kelman, 2012), is the lack of clear connection between disaster-related activities and successful diplomacy. In some cases, disasters influenced already existing diplomacy, as with Greece and Turkey. In other instances, such as the U.S.A. with Cuba and Iran, no discernible connection emerged. In terms of disasters influencing diplomacy, disaster diplomacy appears to have had limited impact.

4.2 *Disaster Diplomacy: What is Success?*

While the phrase 'disaster diplomacy' had been used with limited discussed in earlier work (Dove, 1998; Dove and Khan, 1995; Silverstein, 1999), the first detailed investigation of the phrase's meaning and implementation was by Kelman and Koukis (2000). As Streich and Mislan (2014) describe, this work did not draw on the earlier generation of relevant literature. Using the three case studies of Greece-Turkey (Ker-Lindsay, 2000), Cuba-U.S.A. (Glantz, 2000), and southern Africa (Holloway, 2000) plus a synthesis and analysis by Comfort (2000), Kelman and Koukis (2000) asked 'Do natural disasters induce international cooperation amongst countries that have traditionally been "enemies" '?' (p. 214). Kelman (2012) deconstructs that question, suggesting five ways in which it could be improved.

First, he explains how the term 'natural disasters' is a misnomer, using the line of argument introduced in section 3. Second, the focus on 'disaster' might be too limiting because disaster risk reduction activities could also be pertinent for influencing diplomacy. Third, the focus on 'international cooperation' is an important element of diplomacy and ought to be considered, but other approaches for diplomacy, as explored in section 3, are part of the disasters-politics nexus. Fourth, the term 'enemy' would be easy to misinterpret and could be too harsh a descriptor for many parties involved in diplomatic processes. Finally, it is a yes/no question, whereas interpreting and explaining beyond the mere presence or absence of disaster diplomacy is important for research and foreign policy.

Kelman (2012) revised the disaster diplomacy question to 'how and why disaster-related activities do and do not create peace and reduce conflict' (p. 4) although he also uses 'how and why disaster-related activities do and do not induce cooperation amongst enemies' (p. 13). As a research question, these two statements provide much more insight, determining the mechanisms and reasons by which disaster diplomacy is or is not seen (see also Comfort, 2000). Definitions and understandings are still required for 'peace', 'conflict', 'cooperation', and their interactions. Diplomacy intersects with these processes leading to a broad discussion covering a wide range of case studies, many forms of disaster and disaster risk reduction, and many activities within diplomacy by different parties, confirming the disaster diplomacy hypothesis that 'disaster-related activities can act as a catalyst, but not as a creator, of diplomacy' (p. 14). In an insightful review and analysis with much broader and deeper scope, Streich and Mislan (2014, p. 85) conclude that '(1) Disasters generally do not lead to the initiation of conflict. (2) Disasters generally do not lead to new cooperative processes. (3) Disasters can catalyze or reinforce existing rapprochement processes between conflict-prone dyads.'

Here, this previous research work is extended and applied for foreign policy relevance through the baseline question: Under what circumstances could 'disaster diplomacy' be actively made to succeed or not succeed? By answering this question, more knowledge is provided regarding whether or not to actively enact disaster diplomacy along with possibilities in which disaster response and disaster risk reduction efforts could create or worsen conflict.

To determine the circumstances in which disaster diplomacy succeeds or not, 'success' requires a definition. Based on Kelman (2012) and Streich and Mislan (2014), success could mean that disaster-related activities—that is, disaster response or disaster risk reduction—have catalysed diplomacy with the presumption that the catalysis led to a positive diplomatic outcome which could be a peace deal, augmented diplomatic connections, or further talks. Positive outcomes for disaster-related activities—improved disaster response, more successful emergency management, or increased disaster risk reduction efforts—could also be considered.

Kelman (2012) and Streich and Mislan (2014) confirm that disaster-related activities sometimes catalyse diplomacy in the short-term, but do not create diplomacy and do not affect longer-term endeavours. They further note that disaster-related activities have the potential to act as a catalyst for diplomacy only when already existing conditions support the evolution of the diplomacy. Examples of those conditions could be ongoing negotiations, cultural connections, and trade links, all of which provide connections amongst the parties involved, providing a foundation for further diplomatic developments. The connections could and do occur within any diplomacy activities. The other element of confirming the hypothesis in Kelman (2012) is that any catalysis occurring is witnessed over only weeks or months, a fairly short time frame. Beyond several months and over years, other factors usually supersede any catalysis from disaster response or disaster risk reduction. Other factors include a change in leadership or policy, a preference to retain historical grievances rather than overcoming them, and further disasters.

To a large degree, such analysis takes a snapshot of a situation and views the parties as being passive participants in terms of how disaster-related activities could and would influence diplomacy. Active disaster diplomacy was discussed in Kelman (2012) with a few examples noted, but for the most part, active disaster diplomacy involved speculation and was not thoroughly analysed. Instead, the focus was on whether or not disaster diplomacy would be observed, rather than the circumstances under which it could be deliberately supported or deliberately inhibited. Yet as Streich and Mislan (2014) astutely note, the definition of 'disaster diplomacy' is unclear with often inconsistent descriptions. Policy makers need to know not only what does and could happen, but also how to actively shape events to reach a preferred outcome—and for what exactly they aim.

This statement leads to a further quandary regarding the definition of 'success'. If the desired outcome of a party actively involved in disaster diplomacy is less diplomacy or even increased disaster risk, then the outcome might be achieved and this party could claim success. Other parties might not claim success because they desired a different outcome. The reverse holds. Even if the desired outcome for one party is disaster diplomacy and they work actively towards it, then other parties might oppose that outcome and work actively against it. Success is in the eye of the beholder.

Notwithstanding the acceptance that these different viewpoints and objectives exist, an ideological assumption is made here that fewer disasters, reduced disaster risk, and increased diplomacy are desired outcomes and, if linked, are the indicators for disaster diplomacy's success. Since direct and sole causation of diplomacy or conflict due to disaster response or disaster risk reduction has not yet been shown, the circumstances under which disaster diplomacy could be actively made to succeed or not succeed are explored.

4.3 *Theoretical Notions: Intentionality and Foreseeability*

The disaster diplomacy literature, as one component of the intersection of disasters and politics, concludes from case studies and theoretical developments that disaster response and disaster risk reduction have the potential to catalyse diplomatic processes in the short-term, but not in the long-term, if a pre-existing basis exists for the diplomacy. Yet disaster-related activities do not necessarily lead to more diplomacy. They can be neutral or they can catalyse conflict. Starting from this point, this section examines two theoretical notions applied to disaster diplomacy: intentionality and foreseeability.

As hinted in section 4.2, one of the key theoretical questions not explored extensively is intentionality. In making decisions not to provide aid to, or not to accept aid from, another party (with whom one might have a conflict), is the intention to kill more people, whether of the other party or of one's own citizens? Expressing the intention in these stark terms is not typical, but it is not too far from what has happened. Cuban-Americans in Florida and some American government officials hoped that a disaster in Cuba might destabilise Fidel Castro's regime (Glantz, 2000). Intentionality was present in terms of aiming for more Cuban suffering so that the people would rise up and overthrow the government. The Nicaraguan leader in 1972 would have known that lining his and his friends' pockets with disaster aid would increase Nicaraguans' suffering. Intentionality was present in terms of the leaders not being concerned about their own citizens. With intentionality seeking to cause harm, disaster diplomacy is not expected to succeed because the goal is to avoid the process.

Where disaster diplomacy is not intentionally opposed, is it intentionally promoted? For Greece and Turkey, the earthquakes catalysed the rapprochement, significantly pushing it along—which, in turn, caused trouble unintentionally by pushing it out into the limelight and giving detractors a target. The catalysis itself caught Greek and Turkish leaders by surprise (Ker-Lindsay, 2000, 2007), because they had not been intending to make their diplomatic progress so public so soon. The leaders were caught up in the grassroots and media wave of positive feelings and had to scramble to regain control of the process. Their populace responded intuitively with intentions and expectations of earthquake diplomacy while the leaders would have preferred to move forward with diplomacy at their own, more staid pace.

Perhaps, though, leaders could seize opportunities and be more active in using disaster response and disaster risk reduction to support, rather than to oppose, diplomacy. They could intentionally select disaster diplomacy by responding to a disaster with active diplomacy or by enacting disaster risk reduction activities for the express purpose, whether admitted openly or not, of forging improved diplomacy. If this choice is made, then further case studies are needed to examine how such goals could be pursued and the likelihood of success. The next two sections explore two new disaster diplomacy case studies, focused on disaster risk reduction rather than the more common, previous case studies of disaster response from section 4.1.

In particular, the foreseeability of outcomes from intentional disaster diplomacy efforts needs to be considered. Glantz (2003) applies the concept of foreseeability to the context of climate-related hazards. He highlights the legal definition that 'Foreseeability encompasses not only that which the defendant foresaw, but that which the defendant ought to have foreseen' (Gifis, 195–196), in effect describing accountability for decisions and actions. In the disaster diplomacy context, if an active decision is made to pursue disaster diplomacy—that is, intentionality—how much foreseeability exists regarding its potential success, failure (perhaps making the situation worse), or lack of effect?

Southern African droughts illustrate. During the 1991–1993 drought (Holloway, 2000), the governments of the region and regional organisations were well aware of the food and water situation. They knew the likely consequences, which were foreseeable, so they intentionally responded with coordinated food imports and distribution, preventing the foreseeable drought disaster. The leaders had accountability and held themselves to account by resolving the situation.

In contrast, Zimbabwe received strong warnings in mid-2002 that an El Niño-related drought had a strong likelihood of manifesting in 2003. The warnings mentioned that the drought would exacerbate the food shortages which were already predicted due to previous years of corruption, land ownership changes, and forced changes in farming practices, all reducing nation-wide food production (Glantz and Cullen, 2003). Despite the forecast, which ended up having a high level of accuracy and precision, Zimbabwe's government did not make use of the time they were given in order to avoid a famine (Howard-Hassmann, 2010). A food deficit and hungry population lasted several years, worsened by Zimbabwe's leadership continuing to hamper farming, food distribution, and aid. The catastrophe was foreseeable but was not acted upon—and no mechanism existed for turning foreseeability into accountability.

Many other theoretical notions have been presented in the context of disasters influencing politics. Pelling and Dill (2010) provide one summary, focusing on 'tipping points' (cf. Gladwell, 2000). They also contrast the view of disasters leading to an 'accelerated status quo' in which élites retain control of political processes with the view of disasters being a 'critical juncture' leading to a political step change (p. 22). Two main limitations emerge in applying these theories to the practical world of foreign policy and diplomacy.

First, more options exist than the two provided. In Greece-Turkey disaster diplomacy, the élites lost a significant part of their control over the diplomacy due to the groundswell of non-élite desire to a help a neighbour, so 'accelerated status quo' was not the case. Simultaneously, the earthquakes became one blip amongst many in the long rapprochement process, so the disasters were not a 'critical juncture'. With Cuba-U.S.A., multiple disasters over the decades had no impact. It was not an 'accelerated status quo', merely a 'status quo', which further means no 'critical juncture'.

In fact, the assumption that an 'equilibrium state' (Pelling and Dill, 2010, p. 35) inevitably exists in politics which can be shifted to another equilibrium state is contestable. Cuba more or less held an equilibrium state in politics for 49 years under Fidel Castro. The U.S.A. has rarely had an equilibrium state given its four-year election cycle which includes the Presidential campaign; its mid-term elections which includes Congress; and its off-year elections which can shift the balance of power at local and state levels. Cuba-U.S.A. relations held an equilibrium state in terms of the American trade embargo and mutual hostility, but not in terms of high-level contacts. These waxed and waned according to the interests of power brokers in Washington, D.C., alongside other geopolitical events from the Cuban Missile Crisis in 1962 to Cuban troops in Angola from 1975–1991 to the 11 September 2001 terrorist attacks in the northeastern U.S.A. (Domínguez, 1997; LeoGrande, 2008/2009). In diplomacy, an equilibrium state exists in some contexts and not in others, with both situations interacting.

The second main limitation of Pelling and Dill (2010) is that their theoretical notions are placed alongside others in a flowchart sporting a 'cycle of disaster and political change' (p. 29). As is evident from the discussion of diplomacy's meaning (section 3.5), political interactions are rarely a single, connected line. Instead, multiple interactions are happening at multiple levels, sometimes connected and sometimes not. Segalla's (2012) work on disaster diplomacy in Morocco lucidly identifies the large number of parties involved with different interests working across at least three distinct disasters (floods, the poisoning, and the earthquake). The Americans had simultaneous but not necessarily compatible objectives (supporting Moroccans, reducing the aid budget, keeping Morocco as a Cold War ally, and determining the usefulness of an air base in the country) as did the Moroccans (reducing disaster impacts, asserting their new independence, holding colonialism and post-colonialism accountable or using them as a scapegoats, acquiring aid, and determining with which Cold War powers to ally). Pelling and Dill (2010) acknowledge 'multiple scales' (p. 34) but do not fully engage with or apply them, such as through expanding the flowchart or indicating the possibilities for multiple, interacting flowcharts.

As such, certain theoretical formulations are useful for academic discourse and for providing an entry into disaster-politics interactions. For policy relevance and for determining how disaster diplomacy decisions are made in reality, intentionality and foreseeability are amongst the more practical theoretical notions, so they are used here.

4.4 *Ethical Implications*

Policy makers and practitioners for diplomacy can aim to achieve specific objectives (intentionality), can gather and analyse information and advice to determine potential consequences of actions (foreseeability), and can make active decisions, such as whether or not efforts should be made for disaster diplomacy to succeed (or fail). Even where the explicitly stated objective is to support disaster diplomacy—including through reducing detrimental disaster impacts and through increasing diplomacy—ethical questions arise encompassing the foreseeability of those objectives causing more problems than they solve.

As soon as disaster-related and diplomatic activities are connected, a concern emerges that the failure of one process could lead to failure in other processes. As with Iran and the U.S.A. after the 2003 earthquake, the energy put into and the subsequent failure of disaster diplomacy had the potential to interfere with effective humanitarian aid and swift recovery. While that statement is hypothetical for Iran-U.S.A. interactions, it was seen in reality through Iran's refusal to accept Israeli help, despite Israel having renowned disaster rescue and disaster medicine teams (Bar-Dayan et al., 2000). Israel is also comparatively nearby, so is in a strong position to save lives rapidly in Iran. With Israel, Iran directly connected disaster-related activities and diplomacy, refusing both in tandem. With the U.S.A., Iran separated disaster-related activities and diplomacy, accepting the aid but declining to use it as leverage for higher-level contact. Had the U.S.A. insisted from the beginning that successful disaster diplomacy be a post-earthquake outcome, then Iran might have refused the American aid.

A moral dilemma appears for both sides, not just in 2003 but also in subsequent disasters. For Iran, a decision is needed regarding requesting aid and accepting offers. For the U.S.A., a decision is needed regarding offering and providing aid. Both countries needed to determine if the provision of aid should immediately and explicitly be linked to political topics, such as negotiations over nuclear power and weapons, sanctions, support for combatants in the region, and Israel. If the answer is 'no', then the connections end up being superficial, providing disaster relief as a superficial solution which does strike at root causes of vulnerability, namely long-term political processes. If the answer is 'yes', then the countries become enmeshed in multiple levels of interaction which might distract from immediate needs on the ground. If the answers differ, as appeared to be the case in 2003, then diplomacy can be set back, which was the outcome.

A contrast is seen in 2005 when, after Hurricane Katrina, Iran offered aid which the U.S.A. refused, with no further outcomes apart from the status quo. Perhaps disaster response in the U.S.A. was inhibited by refusing to accept humanitarian aid from Iran, but there was no intimation that acceptance or refusal would be connected with other topics.

When disaster aid is accepted, many situations exist where the aid worsens the circumstances or, at minimum, does not contribute substantively (Anderson, 1999; Terry, 2002). The detrimental impacts of aid are not just political, such as enhancing discrimination, creating dependency, giving power to those controlling the aid, promoting migration away from communities towards aid centres, and perpetuating the vulnerabilities and/or conflicts which caused the disaster in the first place. Post-disaster assistance can also introduce major logistical difficulties, such as the need to allocate money, equipment, and personnel for receiving and distributing assistance; determining equitable distribution, such as assessing needs or providing equal aid; and dealing with inappropriate donations which often include culturally incompatible food, clothing not suited to the local climate, or useless items which have included out-of-date medical drugs and roller blades in a location without paved roads.

Moreover, in earthquakes including in Iran in 2003, the majority of rescuees are pulled from the rubble due to local efforts, before external rescue teams arrive (Alexander, 2007). While foreigners saving people creates good media coverage, noting the importance of disaster imagery for catalysing humanitarian aid (Hutchinson, 2014), and while the rescue of a single life should never be denigrated, disaster-related resources would be far more effective if all rescue teams trained for and responded to nearby disasters only. The money which they set aside for air fares and for living independently in the field (to avoid taxing local food, water, and energy supplies) could be donated to training and equipping local rescue teams.

Yet any external rescue team can potentially form bonds with the communities in which it operates. Stories abound, even if not recorded in the literature, of rescuers staying in touch with rescuees long after the disaster. Speculation leads to ideas that American rescuers (or even Israeli ones, if they were permitted to enter Iran) could form connections with Iranians in need, yielding public diplomacy which ultimately supports bilateral reconciliation years later. The ethics of hoping that such a situation emerges, and then acting on it, are discussed further in section 7.3 as part of a disaster diplomacy research agenda. Since rescuers, professional and non-professional, are sometimes attacked or sued by their rescuees (Krebs, 2003; Weldon, 2010), being rescued does not inevitably form strong bonds or lead to peace-related outcomes.

Nonetheless, speculating about long-term outcomes due to rescue and other forms of humanitarian aid ought to be raised, debated, and discussed, but are unlikely to ever be truly answered because counterfactuals cannot be proven. If the 1999 earthquakes had not happened in Greece and Turkey, or if just one earthquake had struck, would the diplomatic endeavours have moved faster, slower, or at the same overall pace? If Iran had made different decisions after each earthquake regarding aid from Israel, the U.S.A., Egypt, and other countries—and if the U.S.A. had accepted aid from Iran after Hurricane

Katrina—how would Iran's international relations have fared? The process is not linear because these decisions could have affected election results.

Speculating on hypotheticals is important and occurs within this paper. Further case studies to assist with comparative analyses are also important. The next two sections introduce further disaster diplomacy case studies, focusing on disaster risk reduction and exploring how active disaster diplomacy might be suitable for seeking disaster diplomacy success.

5 Case Study: Disease Diplomacy

Much international cooperation exists for health-related topics, including public health diplomacy, using health interventions for foreign policy outcomes, and seeking community cooperation through health initiatives. A 'Journal of Health Diplomacy' was founded in 2013 (http://www.journalofhealthdiplomacy.org) and the advent of 'global health' initiatives has led to examinations of global health diplomacy (for instance, Kevany, 2014). Both directions are examined in terms of how foreign policy can influence health (Kickbusch, 2011) and how health interventions can influence foreign policy (Licina, 2011). The main UN agency dealing with health topics is the World Health Organization (WHO), with 'Health as a Bridge for Peace' (Garber, 2002) being one of their health diplomacy programmes. Another prominent international agency is the US government's Centers for Disease Control and Prevention, which pursues health diplomacy in collaboration with other US government institutions such as the Department of State the Department of Defense.

This section covers the health diplomacy subset of disease diplomacy, examining international efforts to eradicate disease along with vaccination programmes in order to examine any disaster diplomacy outcomes. Both disease eradication (section 5.1) and vaccination programmes (section 5.2) are, in effect, disaster risk reduction since they are about preventing epidemics and pandemics. They also have some links to disaster response, since the diseases exist already and many of the epidemics are occurring over long time scales.

The focus on disease rather than on other health problems, such as chronic conditions and lifestyles, is to ensure that the discussion here sits within disaster diplomacy. An epidemic is defined as 'The occurrence in a community or region of cases of an illness, specific health-related behaviour, or other health-related events clearly in excess of normal expectancy' (WHO, 2007) while a pandemic is, in effect, a large-scale epidemic (Kelly, 2011). Epidemics and pandemics are disasters, with needed links frequently made to disaster response and disaster risk reduction in terms of research, policy, and practice

(Aitsi-Selmi et al., 2015). While there is no clear-cut delineation between health concerns which are and are not a disaster—witness, for instance, obesity continually being labelled as an epidemic and the wider field of non-communicable diseases—the examples here assist in highlighting parallels with other disasters permitting comparators for disaster diplomacy analyses. Section 5.3 brings together many of the topics through discussing health interventions as foreign policy.

5.1 *Disease Eradication*

International cooperation has eradicated a handful of diseases. Following an intensification in 1967 of the programme run by the UN's World Health Organization (WHO) to eliminate smallpox, it was formally declared successful from 1979–1980 (Breman and Arita, 1980). The eradication required intense international cooperation, across dozens of countries accepting protocols for vaccinating against and monitoring for the disease. Cooperation within countries was also needed to overcome barriers raised by civil wars, discrimination against certain groups, and distrust of outsiders.

Fenner (1982) describes how barriers were overcome in India and Ethiopia, including violent conflict in the latter, mainly through household-by-household surveillance and, when infected people were found, isolation. No intimation is made that any conflicts could or should have been solved, or were solved, by the eradication programme. Instead, the description is of medical personnel entering communities and engaging with people in a top-down manner to elicit cooperation, focusing on only smallpox without suggestions of wider considerations.

This approach succeeded. The last known fatality from smallpox occurred in 1978 in the U.K. through an accidental release in a medical laboratory at the University of Birmingham (Cooper, 2006). Samples of the virus are retained in government laboratories in the U.S.A. and Russia and the genome has been sequenced. Planning continues for possible smallpox outbreaks (Ferguson et al., 2003) through a deliberate release, perhaps of a synthesised microbe, with the most likely cause usually claimed to be terrorism. As Casey et al. (2005) and Cooper (2006) describe, in 2002–2003, the U.S.A. decided to vaccinate its military personnel and to voluntarily vaccinate bioterrorism first responders against smallpox, with the latter experiencing three deaths, two permanent disabilities, and ten life-threatening sicknesses from the vaccine.

The smallpox eradication discourse is now highlighting smallpox as a weapon and as part of conflict, whereas before, it did not consider eradication as a potential pathway to peace. Keeping smallpox eradication as an international medical effort with a single objective and not connecting it to wider issues might have been an element in the eradication programme's success. Fenner (1982) goes through eight clinical reasons which made smallpox a prime candidate for eradication, notably that no animals carry the disease, all those infected display symptoms, the virus' infectivity characteristics increase the chance of breaking the infection chain, outbreaks were seasonal providing disease-free months for planning, and the existence of a stable and effective vaccine. No political reasons are emphasised favouring or inhibiting smallpox eradication. Instead, tackling the disease appears to have been viewed as a purely medical problem without related, non-medical outcomes—and perhaps that attitude was a political factor in the campaign's success.

Some similar factors were highlighted for the successful eradication of rinderpest, a virus killing cattle which led to widespread human starvation in areas affected. The campaign started in 1994 and ended in 2010, although eradication was not formally accepted until 2011 (Morens et al., 2011). Earlier eradication efforts had failed meaning that the disease re-emerged, but then a stable, effective vaccine coupled with local, participatory processes led to the eradication programme's success (Mariner et al., 2012).

The balance of social and technical factors is poignant, with the strong emphasis being that eradication could not have succeeded without both approaches combined. As Mariner et al. (2012, p. 1312) write, 'The technical research to develop a thermostable rinderpest vaccine required 2 years to complete, but the social innovation to capture the benefit required more than a decade'. This social innovation refers to the participatory epidemiology used, especially in conflict-ridden areas, effected by training locals to watch for the disease and then community-based services to administer vaccines. Locals included pastoralists who know the land and the communities because they roam. Involving them in the surveillance and vaccination not only avoided their actions supporting transmission but also led to enthusiastic cooperation because they understood and accepted the relevance of the work.

Throughout the rinderpest eradication, the campaign was not used to solve long-standing conflicts in infected locations. Disease diplomacy was not pursued. Instead, the focus of the sociological innovation was eradicating the disease. Part of the eradication programme's success stemmed from that narrow focus. Yet community development which would last long afterwards was inevitably part of the programme. Skills acquired through participatory epidemiology and the connections made with community-based animal health services would not disappear overnight, instead conferring credibility for animal health on those involved and building connections within and amongst communities. It appears that the resulting changes and the development gains are not being monitored directly, meaning that it is hard to attribute long-term outcomes of rinderpest eradication beyond that programme.

Literature on the wars in Ethiopia, Eritrea, and Sudan tends to mention rinderpest in passing or of historical interest. Literature on rinderpest tends to mention violent conflict as one factor amongst many to overcome. The Ethiopian-Eritrean wars of 2000–2002 occurred after the last reported rinderpest case in Ethiopia in 1995, so Ethiopia-Eritrea disaster diplomacy has so far been investigated for only the droughts occurring during the fighting (Kelman, 2012). Overall, little connection has been made between rinderpest and conflict resolution, most likely because little connection occurred. Not attempting any such connection removed the eradication programme from local politics to a degree, helping the community development processes which embraced rinderpest surveillance and vaccinations.

Despite multiple types and scales of conflict within smallpox- and rinderpest-affected areas, the two diseases were eradicated, a process necessitating cooperation across international boundaries and within communities, irrespective of any form of conflict. If, indeed, part of the political success of the eradication programmes was due to separating the vaccinations from conflicts, then disease diplomacy lessons could be applied to other, ongoing disease eradication programmes.

The most prominent disease eradication programmes currently are dracunculiasis (Guinea worm disease), measles, and polio. Guinea worm is a parasite that enters people when they drink contaminated water. The eradication campaign started in the early 1980s with the key step being to provide safe drinking water, but monitoring and surveillance are important too which incorporates working with infected people to rid themselves of the parasite without reintroducing it into water supplies (Biswas et al., 2013). From the World Health Organization (http://www.who.int/dracunculiasis/en), cases are declining quickly. In 1990, twenty countries were endemic, but there are only four as of mid-2015: Chad, Ethiopia, Mali and South Sudan.

All four countries have experienced major conflicts during the dracunculiasis eradication programme. Studies directly link violent and political conflict to infectious disease outbreaks (for example, Beyrer et al., 2007) including dracunculiasis (Hopkins et al., 2000). Biswas et al. (2013) identify conflicts as restricting access for health workers addressing dracunculiasis and forcing people to flee the fighting, potentially bringing dracunculiasis to other locations and across international borders. They further highlight the importance of a ceasefire in Sudan, labelled as both 1995 (p. 6) and 1996 (p. 9), as being a turning point for identifying cases in that country.

Yet despite the emphasis on social and political interventions creating the campaign's success (Barry, 2006; Biswas et al., 2013), the literature shies away from discussing the possibilities for using dracunculiasis eradication as a conflict reduction or conflict resolution measure or as a mechanism for bringing together parties in conflict. Similar observations are seen for measles and polio, as discussed under ongoing vaccine diplomacy in the next section.

5.2 *Vaccine Diplomacy*

From the beginning of measles eradication efforts, which would be based entirely on vaccination, the case was made on clinical and economic bases (Foege, 1982; Hopkins et al., 1982). Diplomatic challenges and diplomatic outcomes, such as prospects for measles eradication to be an impetus towards conflict reduction or conflict resolution, were not discussed. In 2010, measles was accepted as being eradicable with a target date of 2020, a programme which in 2012 morphed into the Measles and Rubella Initiative. The focus continued to be on the clinical aspects and expected success of the vaccination campaigns without links to wider development issues.

While challenges to successful measles eradication are still emphasised as being conflict, displaced populations, and political troubles (Roy et al., 2014)—that is, entirely social rather than medical—suggestions are not being made regarding possibilities for using measles eradication as a conduit towards tackling these social issues. Furthermore, the lack of expected progress in moving towards measles eradication is attributed primarily to conflict and poor health systems (Durrheim and Dahl-Regis, 2014). If peace and health systems are a prerequisite for measles eradication, then would it make more sense to focus on diplomacy in order to permit robust health systems which would then permit measles eradication?

For polio eradication, which started in 1988, the literature tells a parallel tale, focusing on eradication as a medical challenge while acknowledging that eradication has not been successful due to politics, namely conflict. Gostin (2014) details killings and expulsions of polio vaccination workers in order to explain that 'polio eradication requires a political, not merely a technical, solution. Although we have the scientific know-how to eradicate polio, what is required are diplomacy and the public acceptance of mass vaccination programs' (p. 415). Garon and Orenstein (2015) mull over the strategy of placing less focus on a single-disease vaccination campaign in order to favour overall child health care in order to improve medical access to conflict zones. The two remaining countries where polio is endemic, Afghanistan and Pakistan, are wracked by conflict. Some populations in those countries maintain strong suspicion against vaccination campaigns, notably because hepatitis B vaccination was used in Pakistan as a cover for collecting DNA samples as part of the plan to kill Osama bin Laden.

As with measles, the literature does not suggest that the polio eradication campaign is capable of bringing peace to conflict areas nor are wider dimensions of diplomacy discussed as possible outcomes from the efforts. In fact, during the Cold War, the polio vaccine was developed and distributed internationally through American-Soviet collaboration (Hotez, 2001ab) with no intimation that it could or should have contributed to solving the Cold War or even to reducing tensions.

Yet ceasefires have been negotiated to permit UN vaccination campaigns in several countries, for example Afghanistan, the Democratic Republic of Congo, Liberia, and Sierra Leone (Hotez, 2001ab). In every single instance, as corroborated by Hotez (2001a), the lobbying to achieve a vaccine-related ceasefire and the vaccination campaign itself did not lessen the conflict. Instead, the fighting continued once each ceasefire had ended. It seemed that no parties involved truly sought peace, so they were content to permit the medical intervention knowing that it would not affect their military means. It is conceivable that certain parties welcomed the lull in the fighting to rest, regroup, and restock—or even worse that they hoped the vaccinations would provide them with healthier soldiers, although there is no evidence for or against this contention.

Bush (2004) is more optimistic, referring to immunization days in Somalia, the Democratic Republic of Congo, and Sri Lanka as having created ceasefires and controlling polio, potentially to the point of eradication in Sri Lanka. He writes 'The success of this initiative illustrates that children's health can become a superordinate goal around which interests can coverage across battle lines to induce the cooperation necessary for immunization campaigns', further citing 'Cambodia, El Salvador, Lebanon, and the Philippines' (Bush, 2004, p. 34). These words match exactly what has been presented so far: vaccine diplomacy yields a ceasefire for immunization only, with no further outcomes. Eleven years later, Bush's (2004) contention that 'immunization days may have a positive impact on efforts to end conflicts' is not supported by subsequent events. DRC and Somalia remain embroiled in war. Sri Lanka's peace was achieved militarily, as presented in section 1. While vaccine campaigns in war zones continue and may be supporting disease eradication, they are not bringing peace or supporting long-term diplomacy.

This discussion neither condemns vaccine diplomacy nor criticises the lack of connection of vaccination and disease eradication with conflict resolution. Conversely, had vaccination and disease eradication been forcefully linked to conflict resolution, then the parties involved might have denied or interfered with the vaccination and disease eradication efforts. Additionally, long-term analyses of the effects of the ceasefires on the conflicts were not found, with the literature instead relying on the assumption that vaccination programmes and conflict resolution are separate. Determining what would have happened in each conflict without the disease-related ceasefires is not possible.

Vaccine diplomacy has been labelled and implemented as an active disaster diplomacy measure, although without success so far. Hotez (2004) believes that the U.S.A. should pursue a vaccine diplomacy programme, providing these health interventions as part of foreign policy. It has been attempted with North Korea. In 2009, South Korea sent swine flu medicine to North Korea without any substantive diplomatic consequence, positive or negative.

5.3 *Health Interventions as Foreign Policy*

Neither disease eradication nor vaccine diplomacy has led to clear-cut disaster diplomacy successes. Nor has it seemed that extensive efforts have been made to use disease for active disaster diplomacy, despite numerous calls to do so, especially in the realms of 'global health diplomacy' and 'global health as foreign policy' (Kevany, 2014); in effect, using health topics for public diplomacy. Overall, intentionality to support disease diplomacy is absent. Conversely, the separation of international disease-related programmes from diplomatic efforts, especially in conflict zones, might be a factor in programmes' success. Perhaps it is foreseeable that, to succeed, disease-related programmes should not be linked to conflict reduction or conflict resolution. Perhaps, the parties are actively pursuing their approach based on that foreseeability rather than on ignorance.

Historically, health diplomacy was applied but with little long-term success. Edward Jenner, the English inventor of the smallpox vaccine, became so venerated that he mediated prisoner exchanges between England and France in the nineteenth century (Hotez, 2001a), but with no recorded further outcomes related to diplomacy. Customary international humanitarian law based in the Geneva and Hague Conventions, and many countries' military manuals, support ceasefires to permit the removal from the battlefield and care of wounded soldiers. Wars did not end as a result.

Nonetheless, Yim et al. (2009bc) argue that health diplomacy has been the most effective manner of the U.S.A. engaging with North Korea, for helping the North Korean population survive famine and for American NGOs to receive permission to enter and operate in North Korea. Similarly, Hotez and Thompson (2009) argue that a strong way of making overseas populations more friendly towards the U.S.A. would be vaccine and wider health diplomacy, so it should be part of the American foreign policy. An added advantage they raise is the cost-effectiveness, in terms of prevention rather than response and in terms of positive impacts compared to other foreign aid interventions.

It is unclear why vaccine diplomacy should be cheaper and have more positive impacts on recipient populations than an American foreign policy which avoids providing aid to governments which oppress their own people. By curtailing military aid and by getting involved in fewer overseas wars, less American tax money would be spent and fewer people affected by violent conflict would identify the U.S.A., rightly or wrongly, as the aggressor. Hotez and Thompson (2009) accept the problem that defence and military spending by the American government is orders of magnitude greater than its expenditure on non-military aid, including development work and health diplomacy. In the absence of substantive reductions in defence and military spending, or in the absence of substantive changes in the American government's overseas military policy, it may be that health diplomacy is an important option.

Nonetheless, Hotez's (2010) vision for improved American foreign policy towards and relations with Islamic countries based on health diplomacy does not recognise that the diplomacy and the bilateral relations might fail if either party, or both, are disinterested in diplomacy. While this possibility should not necessarily preclude efforts, unless there is evidence that health diplomacy would do more harm than good, greater awareness of the realism surrounding diplomatic interactions would assist in judging the potential effectiveness of health diplomacy for American foreign policy.

One observation is that the majority of literature advocating for active use of health diplomacy as a foreign policy tool comes from American writers promoting it for American foreign policy. The U.S.A. has major health and health systems problems of its own. The country requires significant interventions to get its own population up to a healthy standard. Despite new legislation in recent years, the U.S.A. still has a long way to go before the entire population has access to good quality and affordable health care (if that is a desired goal). Scope therefore exists for health diplomacy to be initiated by other countries for the U.S.A., if the other countries aim for public diplomacy with the American people.

After Hurricane Katrina, Cuba's aid offer included more than 1,000 doctors and several tonnes of medical supplies; China offered medical experts; India included medicine, a medical team and water purification systems in their offer; Mexico sent medical supplies delivered by Mexican army vehicles crossing the border; and Russia suggested supplying medicines and drinking water (Kelman, 2007). Considering that most offers were not accepted and that the U.S.A.'s relations with other countries did not change as a result of Hurricane

Katrina disaster diplomacy (Kelman, 2007), medical diplomacy failed in this case study.

The health interventions reviewed in sections 5.1 and 5.2, though, had a level of effectiveness. Programmes were implemented, had a positive impact on the ground, and achieved their aims such as disease eradication and vaccinations, but few tangible outcomes were documented beyond the specific health-related aims. Intentionality was focused on health outcomes, not diplomatic outcomes, and success resulted in those health outcomes. The focus on the health results rather than on any outcomes beyond health has been suggested here as potentially being a key factor in the programmes' success. Active efforts to expand the success to diplomacy could scupper both the health interventions and the diplomacy. Furthermore, where health programmes have not yet reached completion—such as dracunculiasis, polio, measles, and rubella eradication (although the first two are close)—the literature explains that inadequate financing is the main cause of the lack of completion, rather than wider political or diplomatic factors.

Thus, the question is raised that if more efforts were put towards diplomacy and diplomatic outcomes, could increased support lead to increased financing? Other disaster diplomacy case studies provide cautionary tales. For Ethiopia-Eritrea's drought diplomacy and Cuba-U.S.A.'s wide-reaching disaster diplomacy (Glantz, 2000; Kelman, 2012), political prominence did not yield either disaster-related or diplomatic-related success. For the earthquakes in Greece and Turkey, heightened prominence led to a backlash against the diplomacy (Ker-Lindsay, 2000, 2007). Conversely, for drought in southern African, the prominence of the diplomacy proceeding irrespective of the drought supported the drought diplomacy and successful disaster risk reduction (Holloway, 2000). Whilst the advocates for more formal and prominent disease diplomacy are suggesting a legitimate pathway, care is needed that it does not backfire especially given that the backfiring is foreseeable based on existing knowledge and previous case studies.

Nevertheless, it is unclear the extent to which networks or links have formed and have been pushed forward through disease diplomacy which might have resulted in diplomatic outcomes beyond the health interventions. Even when pursuing health outcomes as independently of diplomatic outcomes as feasible, further diplomatic consequences might manifest. Donors, such as the Carter Centre and the Bill and Melinda Gates Foundation, could make further in-country political connections and build influence. A low-level official or community worker whose child is saved by the health intervention could rise to be a senior civil servant or political leader—or the child might do so. Tracking this form of results over the long-term has not been found in the literature. These subtle outcomes could require decades to appear and would be influenced by a myriad of other factors.

6 Case Study: Climate Change Diplomacy

Much international cooperation exists for understanding and dealing with climate change, bilaterally and multilaterally. The cooperation occurs in many ways, including scientific/technical collaboration and diplomats negotiating international treaties. These activities are often referred to as 'climate change diplomacy'.

From a disaster diplomacy framing, the climate change diplomacy question investigated in this section becomes how and why dealing with climate change does or does not influence peace and conflict. From the perspective of this paper, the aspect investigated is the circumstances under which climate change diplomacy could be actively made to succeed or not succeed. Climate change is defined and placed within disaster-related activities in section 6.1. Section 6.2 explores the two main activities for dealing with climate change, mitigation and adaptation, as disaster diplomacy processes leading to discussion of success factors. Finally, section 6.3 covers the specific topic of migration potentially linked to climate change.

6.1 *Climate Change: A Creeping Environmental Change*

Creeping environmental changes (also labelled as creeping environmental phenomena and creeping environmental problems) are small changes or trends cumulating to create a major problem which becomes apparent as a crisis only after crossing a specific threshold (Glantz, 1994ab). Climate change is a creeping environmental changes, as is desertification and salinization of water supplies. These changes significantly impact all spatial scales, from local to planetary, so they frequently cross borders. Creeping environmental changes can thus potentially become disasters affecting large swathes across multiple jurisdictions, sometimes requiring a coordinated response, and so they become useful disaster diplomacy cases.

One example is the Aral Sea's human-induced changes over decades (Glantz, 1999). The Aral Sea was in the U.S.S.R. and is now shared by Kazakhstan and Uzbekistan. The Caspian Sea has experienced a similar level of changes and was bordered by the U.S.S.R. and Iran, but is now surrounded by Azerbaijan, Iran, Kazakhstan, Russia, and Turkmenistan. Another example is the impact of precipitation changes under climate change on Fouta Djalon, the headwaters in Guinea from where the Niger, Senegal, and Gambia Rivers begin before flowing through several countries which use the waters for irrigation and drinking. Lessons from these case studies include how early warning for long-term threats would not necessarily positively impact the diplomatic situation and how a useful form of cooperation with respect to creeping environmental problems occurs through scientific and technological processes, such as basic research and operational forecasting. Additionally, transboundary management of these creeping environmental changes can become prominent even when bilateral or multilateral relations are not the overriding influence on the political or environmental situation.

Contemporary climate change is one global creeping environmental change. Climate refers to 'average weather, or more rigorously, as the statistical description in terms of the mean and variability of relevant quantities over a period of time ranging from months to thousands or millions of years. The classical period for averaging these variables is 30 years' (IPCC, 2013–2014: 5). Examining changes in climate therefore encompasses trends, cycles, and baseline shifts.

In referring to contemporary climate change, two principal definitions exist. The UN body responsible for assessing and synthesising climate change science so that a political consensus is reached by governmental members is the UN's Intergovernmental Panel on Climate Change (IPCC). The first IPCC assessment was published in 1990 with the latest one being released in 2013–2014 (IPCC, 2013–2014). The IPCC's (2013–2014, p. 5) definition of climate change is 'a change in the state of the climate that can be identified (for instance, by using statistical tests) by changes in the mean and/or the variability of its properties, and that persists for an extended period, typically decades or longer. Climate change may be due to natural internal processes or external forcings such as modulations of the solar cycles, volcanic eruptions, and persistent anthropogenic changes in the composition of the atmosphere or in land use.'

Meanwhile, the main UN treaty addressing climate change is the United Nations Framework Convention on Climate Change (UNFCCC) which defines climate change to be 'a change of climate which is attributed directly or indirectly to human activity that alters the composition of the global atmosphere and which is in addition to natural climate variability observed over comparable time periods' (UNFCCC, 1992, Article 1, Paragraph 2). The difference in definitions is that the UN's scientific process examines all changes to the climate irrespective of their origin while the UN's policy process considers only climate change from human origins.

The human origins of climate change are twofold: emitting greenhouse gases into the atmosphere and reducing greenhouse gas absorption from the atmosphere (IPCC, 2013–2014). Human activities release greenhouse gases, most notably carbon dioxide but also including several other gases, by burning fossil fuels to generate electricity and to power vehicles, as well as livelihood activities such as raising livestock herds. These gases accumulate in the atmosphere and then trap reflected solar radiation, raising the planet's average temperature and affecting the planet's climate. The vast majority of emissions have been from larger and more affluent countries, including Australia, Canada, China, India, Russia, the U.K., and the U.S.A.

Human-induced changes that reduce the planet's ability to absorb these greenhouse gases reinforce the impact of the emissions. Widespread deforestation and other land use changes mean that trees and other vegetation absorb and store less greenhouse gases. While much of these land use changes have been witnessed in less affluent countries, activities such as rainforest destruction occur primarily to serve consumer demand in the richer countries (Butler and Laurance, 2008). Oceans absorb some carbon dioxide, which reacts with water to make an acid. More carbon dioxide in the air means more acidic oceans, potentially harming marine and coastal ecosystems.

Many feedbacks within the climate system emerge, both contributing to and reducing climate change. As oceans warm, their ability to absorb carbon dioxide is affected. Ash injected into the stratosphere from large volcanic eruptions block sunlight, although the impact seen so far has tended to fade after some years. The effect of clouds is difficult to model, whereas the loss of glaciers and ice sheets through melting reduces the amount of sunlight reflected away from earth. Melting permafrost seems likely to release natural greenhouse gases trapped within it.

Despite the complexities and uncertainties, the science is clear overall that Earth is undergoing a rapid, global, average warming with a significant contribution from human activities. The science is also clear regarding the projected impacts on humans, particularly in terms of influencing the hazard component of disasters (see section 3.1 for the differentiation between hazard and vulnerability).

Warmer air holds more water vapour, leading to the potential for more intense downpours and more intense storms, even while the frequency of some storms such as hurricanes and cyclones is expected to decrease due to climate change (Knutson et al., 2010; Mohapatra et al., 2015). Reduced storm frequency and other changes in precipitation patterns could lead to more water shortages, even if floods increase as precipitation intensity increases.

In places where it snows or where people rely on snowmelt as part of their fresh water supply, complications can emerge. If less snow falls due to higher air temperatures, then more precipitation falls as rain and less snowmelt-related water will be available. Yet as glaciers and ice sheets melt under warmer temperatures, that might increase fresh water flow—until they are gone. While less predictability, more volatility, and wider ranges for weather are expected under climate change, it is hard to make highly specific local projections, apart from the fact that people need to prepare for major changes to weather patterns.

Other projected hazard-related impacts of climate change include rising ocean acidity, mentioned earlier, and rising sea levels (IPCC, 2013–2014). A global average sea-level rise on the order of roughly one metre seems likely because ocean water expands as it warms. If large ice sheets in Greenland and Antarctica melt, then sea-level could rise by several metres, putting major cities and many low-lying islands at risk of inundation. Warmer climates around the world are also expected to radically alter ecosystems and possibly bring human, animal, and plant diseases into locations where they have only rarely appeared before. Geophysical explanations are provided for how climate change might potentially impact earthquakes and volcanoes (McGuire, 2010).

As per the discussion in section 3, a hazard such as a storm or an epidemic is only one part of the disaster equation. The other part is vulnerability. Climate change alone is not enough to cause a disaster, but climate change as a major hazard driver at the global level is a transboundary creeping environmental change and so is suitable for disaster diplomacy analysis. In particular, because climate change and other creeping environmental changes manifest slowly, they give time on the order of decades to deal with the identified challenge. They should be ideal for slow, careful diplomatic processes, working to bring together all parties to target and solve the problem. The next section examines the two main processes existing to deal with climate change, mitigation and adaptation, both of which have mechanisms at international diplomatic levels.

6.2 *Mitigation and Adaptation as Disaster Diplomacy Processes*

According to classifications from IPCC and UNFCCC, two activities are pursued to deal with climate change. Climate change mitigation is human activities reducing greenhouse gas sources or increasing their absorption from the atmosphere. Examples of reducing greenhouse gas sources are reducing electricity demand and using vehicles less. Examples of increasing greenhouse gas uptake are planting trees and removing carbon dioxide from the atmosphere to store it underground as a gas, as a supercritical fluid (neither gas nor liquid), or in mineral form—plus, masonry for buildings can be used to lock in carbon dioxide.

Climate change adaptation is 'The process of adjustment to actual or expected climate and its effects…adaptation seeks to moderate harm or exploit beneficial opportunities' (IPCC, 2013–2014, p. 1). This definition of 'adaptation' is what humanity has been doing for millennia with all hazards and all hazard drivers; that is, adjusting to the environment to avoid harm and to reap the rewards. Examples are building shelter from adverse weather and planting crops which thrive in the microclimates and climates where they are planted. With respect to climate change, adaptation provides little which is new and all such actions are encompassed within the definition of disaster risk reduction given in section 3. As the climate warms, highland farmers might need to use more lowland crops with higher temperatures creeping up to their elevation. As floods and storms intensify and as seas rise, buildings at the edge of a floodplain or coastline might need to be moved from any encroaching waters. Such adjustments have always been made as, respectively, local climates or floodplains changed, with these actions being part of disaster risk reduction.

Despite the explicit separation of mitigation and adaptation in IPCC and UNFCCC processes, little reason exists to keep them apart. Many have recognised the strong overlaps and connections, bringing together mitigation and adaptation to deal with climate change in places such as Vietnam (Dang et al., 2003) and the Sahel (Nyong et al., 2007). This work and other frameworks (for example, Glantz, 2003) demonstrate how IPCC and UNFCCC processes have also separated climate change into its own silo and sector, even though climate change mitigation is simply one aspect of pollution prevention and climate change adaptation is simply one aspect of disaster risk reduction (Kelman et al., 2015). Consequently, dealing with climate change sits as a subset within sustainable development.

Because climate change is one hazard driver amongst many and climate change adaptation sits within disaster risk reduction, the disaster diplomacy principles can be applied to climate change adaptation. The links between adaptation and mitigation mean that some climate change mitigation activities are enveloped as well, even though climate change mitigation is not strictly disaster risk reduction, but pollution prevention.

The climate change diplomacy question is then: Under what circumstances could 'climate change diplomacy' be actively made to succeed or not succeed? Due to the disaster diplomacy framework adopted for this paper, this question diverges from the extensive literature in 'climate diplomacy' and 'climate change diplomacy' (for example, Boas, 2015) which examines the mechanics of seeking international treaties related to climate change. The most prominent mechanism is the UNFCCC process which started out focusing on mitigation but which now covers parts of adaptation. IPCC provides the political and governmental consensus of climate change science which is used to support international treaties. Thus, mitigation and adaptation are represented in the

UN principally by IPCC and UNFCCC processes. The focus now in the rest of this section is how and why the IPCC and UNFCCC mechanics, treaties, agencies, and processes do and do not influence diplomacy for parties in conflict.

Parties to UNFCCC and members of IPCC include Cuba, India, Iran, Israel, Pakistan, and the U.S.A. North Korea is party to UNFCCC, but is not an IPCC member. At UNFCCC and IPCC meetings, all parties make statements and engage in debates, meaning that these countries accept the others' presence and deal with the topic on the table, namely climate change. Irrespective of diplomatic disputes, or in some cases even irrespective of formal diplomatic recognition, all IPCC members have signed off on five assessments since 1990, along with several other IPCC reports, and each of UNFCCC's twenty-one Conferences of the Parties up until the end of 2015 has issued a declaration, also requiring numerous meetings before each formal Conference of the Parties.

Having these venues available to interact has not led to any evidence of new diplomacy being created. Climate change influencing some hazards and climate change bringing together all these countries to negotiate via UNFCCC did not ingratiate Iran into accepting post-earthquake aid from Israel nor help Ethiopia and Eritrea collaborate during their war and drought nor lead to India and Pakistan towards forging peace in order to deal with cyclones and floods. Glantz (2000) analyses Cuba and the U.S.A. concluding that no climate change diplomacy resulted between those two countries. Instead, in terms of climate change's effects, it appears that the countries navigate each other in the contexts of IPCC and UNFCCC, addressing the business relevant for those venues, yet neither wishing for nor seeking any spillover outside of those venues.

This observation is not judging the situation. The lack of climate change diplomacy and the intentionality towards this absence might have advantages. By focusing on climate change only in IPCC and UNFCCC venues, the countries ensure that IPCC and UNFCCC business is completed. Efforts to insert wider topics or to connect IPCC and UNFCCC issues to topics beyond these organisations' strict mandates could scuttle the work of IPCC and UNFCCC. When signing up to either of these institutions, the members and parties agree to the rules and mandates. Attempting other tasks within the venues could jeopardise a country's input into and influence in these venues. By focusing on targeted mandates, IPCC and UNFCCC ensure that they complete their required work on climate change despite the large, diverse membership and despite wider disagreements and conflicts. The lack of IPCC and UNFCCC climate change diplomacy within the disaster diplomacy framing could lead to the functionality of these institutions.

Functionality and adhering to mandates does not necessarily entail diplomatic success. Despite over two decades of UNFCCC Conferences of the Parties and IPCC work, a legally binding substantive global treaty to address climate change still does not exist, despite clear intentionality from many parties towards it. The main international climate change treaty, the Kyoto Protocol which was signed in 1997 and entered into force in 2005, commits some countries to reducing their net greenhouse gas emissions with targets now extended to 2020, but it is analysed as being ineffective and counterproductive (Kutney, 2014; Rosen, 2015). The Paris Agreement, signed on 12 December 2015, has few specific timeframes for achieving substantive results on climate change, while the most effective measures listed in the agreement are not legally binding. Consequently, although IPCC and UNFCCC might function as processes within their fixed mandates and with many parties having intentionality for a substantive treaty, they have not yet succeeded diplomatically in achieving effective action on climate change mitigation or on climate change adaptation, nor have other diplomatic outcomes been realised.

For instance, had the IPCC and UNFCCC climate change processes been used to effect wider diplomatic reconciliation, then American and Israeli desert irrigation techniques and technologies, helpful for climate change adaptation in areas of increasing drought, could have supported Iran's climate change adaptation. Meanwhile, Iran's long history of obtaining water from the desert (Jackson, 2001) could have lessons for Israel and the U.S.A., supporting those countries' climate change adaptation. India's rural electrification with renewable energy has much to offer Pakistan for climate change mitigation (Bhutto et al., 2014). There is no guarantee that any such efforts would have succeeded, but the structures of IPCC and UNFCCC more or less precluded the attempt.

In the end, IPCC and UNFCCC might perhaps be only box-ticking exercises to fulfil their mandates without querying the effectiveness or usefulness of those mandates. For example, research has long existed (e.g. Burns and Flam, 1987) which would question the effectiveness of top-down international agreements, legally binding or not, to create the behavioural change needed for sustainable development. In fact, climate change adaptation and climate change mitigation have both displayed many successes outside the UN, including at national and sub-national levels especially when placed within wider sustainable development activities rather than remaining isolated as purely climate change activities (Waage and Yap, 2015).

Even while IPCC has brought some parts of climate change science onto the world stage and substantially increased awareness of climate change's projected impacts, it has also served as a lightning rod for criticisms. By aiming to undermine the IPCC's work and by convincing themselves that they have done so, critics seem to feel that they have undermined all of climate change science, argued successfully against any climate change mitigation, averted the need for climate change adaptation, and obviated the UNFCCC's work. As such, a process which arguably had some successes initially in raising awareness and galvanising attempted action by joining forces through a formalised intergovernmental process ends up being victimised by the same structure which brought those initial successes.

The end result, as with other disaster diplomacy case studies, is no identified creation of new climate change diplomacy through the IPCC or UNFCCC processes. Moreover, in contrast to some other disaster diplomacy case studies, little catalysis appears to have occurred. Instead, the processes were set up to confine any possibilities for climate change diplomacy outcomes and succeeded in doing so.

6.3 *Climate Change Diplomacy and Migration*

Although little climate change diplomacy seems likely at the international negotiations, climate change diplomacy beyond those processes could be feasible. The topic of climate change migration or so-called 'climate change refugees' is frequently raised as a cross-border climate change concern. The majority of detailed literature investigating this issue (with some examples from a vast collection being Felli and Castree, 2012; Hartmann, 2010; and Nicholson, 2014) concludes, in summary, that (i) direct, causal pathways from climate change to migration-related or non-migration-related decisions are rare; (ii) neither migration nor non-migration should not be problematized, but the advantages and difficulties of each should be recognised; and (iii) the chances are low for major conflicts arising due to interactions between climate change and migration.

None of these studies denies that some communities are planning relocation only due to climate change, such as in Papua New Guinea (Connell, 1997) and Alaska (Bronen and Chapin III, 2013). Nor does this work deny that migration of all forms can cause, prevent, or resolve violent conflict at times. Instead, the literature recognises and accepts that many people in low-lying coastlines, including island communities, might need to move due to climate change impacts, but that many factors influence migration and non-migration decisions. Those decisions can be planned and supported. Due to lack of evidence and lack of theoretical corroboration so far, this body of literature certainly disputes the inevitability of large swathes of climate migrants and the inevitability of conflict resulting from them.

Is it possible, then, that planning and supporting migration or non-migration which has climate change as a major driver could be an opportunity for further diplomacy? That is, could climate change diplomacy be actively enacted (in other words, intentionality) for any changes in migration patterns linked to climate change impacts? In addition to starting dialogue regarding where migrants might move to, the opportunity could be used to bring together parties for addressing climate change mitigation and other sustainable development topics alongside any conflicts. As one possibility, where territory or borders are disputed, finding resettlement locations could hypothetically be an impetus towards a resolution in which the migrants are permitted to settle in and own the disputed territory.

Kiribati, a Pacific island state, purchased land from Fiji in 2014, stating that it would be for resettling when climate change makes much of Kiribati uninhabitable. Maldives, an Indian Ocean island state, had a newly elected President in 2008 who publicised one of his goals as being to save funds in order to purchase land from another country to resettle Maldivians due to climate change's impacts. No new diplomacy emerged from either initiative and neither plan has had much success. The Maldivian plan faded from the spotlight after 2008 and then the President was ousted in 2012, putting a damper on many of his climate change related projects. Discussions on Kiribati's plan indicate confusion regarding the real purpose of the purchase and the viability of developing the land for settlement (Korauaba, 2015).

Disaster diplomacy analyses, displaying a lack of success in previous case studies, curtail thoughts that other efforts, now or into the future, would lead to proactive assistance for those migrating or not migrating due to climate change. Without any evidence for successful disaster diplomacy so far including for climate change diplomacy, foreseeability suggests that, irrespective of intentionality, few expectations are justifiable regarding the use of diplomacy and forethought to resolve climate change linked changes to migration before a crisis erupts. The same conclusion applies to using those connections for wider diplomatic processes.

Entirely precluding the possibility would be presumptuous. There is a chance that migration or non-migration connected with climate change could yield the first known successful disaster diplomacy case study so far, especially if conditions were actively created and pushed to make that happen.

While such speculation is interesting, the reality appears to be the same as for other migration case studies involving strong environmental influences (for instance, Forced Migration Review, 2008). That is, significant action is absent until migration or non-migration becomes forced (e.g. nomads being forced to remain in one location due to a flood or drought), after which diplomatic outcomes from the migration-related decision can be conflict, cooperation, or no effect. Rather than planning ahead and providing adequate support, it appears that people moving or not moving principally due to climate change will suffer the same squalor which so many others have experienced when an environmental hazard or hazard driver forces them to move or to stay (Anderson, 1999; Terry, 2002).

Would there be any way to learn from the past in order to try to prepare for any climate change connected migration or non-migration decisions? Could such action be balanced with the need to avoid expending too many resources in case forced migration or non-migration decisions do not manifest? It appears not. Many politicians from the countries whose populations are most expected to have to move due to climate change have been raising these concerns since the topic first became politically prominent at the Small States Conference on Sea Level Rise, held from 14–18 November 1989 on Malé, the capital of Maldives (http://www.islandvulnerability.org/slr1989.html). This conference was held even before IPCC had delivered its first report and before UNFCCC was formally founded.

Much of the work and declarations from 1989 remain relevant today, suggesting that little changes have resulted, despite plenty of science being published on the topic since then. As with other disaster diplomacy case studies, it seems that for climate change diplomacy and migration-related decisions in practice, substantive action will be taken only once a crisis manifests.

7 Disaster Diplomacy for Connecting Policy Makers and Researchers

In previous sections, disaster diplomacy theory was described and placed in the context of its implications for foreign policy, with contributions from two new case studies. One fundamental thread throughout is that both disaster and diplomacy are processes occurring over multiple scales with multiple people and institutions involved. Consequently, exploring the meaning of 'success' for disaster diplomacy and its implications for foreign policy means accepting multiple processes occurring in tandem, covered by section 7.1. The implications for policy makers in the context of foreign policy are described in section 7.2 followed by section 7.3's research agenda outlining some of the gaps to be explored.

7.1 *Disaster Diplomacy Processes*

The two case studies in sections 5 and 6 corroborate the previous disaster diplomacy conclusions, given in section 4, that disaster-related activities sometimes catalyse diplomacy in the short-term, but not over the long-term, while disaster-related activities have not been shown to create new diplomacy. This section uses the empirical evidence to explain the multi-scalar, multi-faceted processes of disaster diplomacy, rather than expecting disaster diplomacy to be a specific product or outcome. The material interrogates the meaning of 'success' for disaster diplomacy, being realistic about what a disaster diplomacy framing could and could not provide.

The case studies presented in sections 5 and 6 are global in spatial scale and cover decades in temporal scale. Some elements of vaccine diplomacy are about temporary ceasefires for quick vaccination campaigns, yet the main case study investigation covers disease eradication as a global goal, the successes of which were achieved, and continue to be pursued, on a decadal timeframe. For climate change, the focus is on IPCC and UNFCCC, depicting global scale approaches to disaster diplomacy for addressing the challenge of climate change over decades.

Other case studies with a significant literature, as reviewed in section 4, have tended to involve hazards which are shorter in time scales and smaller in space scales, even while vulnerability is always long-term operating at multiple spatial scales. Greece and Turkey's disaster diplomacy, as well as that of India and Pakistan, revolved around earthquakes. Earthquakes occur locally, sometimes with regional impacts, over a time period of minutes at the longest. Cuba-U.S.A. disaster diplomacy has occurred mainly with respect to weather, in which hurricanes are regional in spatial scale, although manifesting and disappearing in days. Tsunami diplomacy for Aceh and Sri Lanka, the case study in sections 1 and 8, involved a hazard appearing suddenly and dissipating after several hours after having affected a large region. The drought diplomacy case studies envelop a large region with drought ramping up and down over months into a few years.

From disease diplomacy and climate change diplomacy, as presented here, similar outcomes are witnessed for these global, long-term hazards. If policy makers have the intentionality of seeking disaster diplomacy, then involvement with global institutions and patience over a long timeframe will not necessarily confer the disaster diplomacy success which they seek. The foreseeability of disaster diplomacy is that diplomacy outcomes are not expected from disaster-related activities, irrespective of the space and time scales considered. In fact, policy makers need to consider circumstances in which disaster diplomacy efforts worsen a diplomatic situation, as with Greece-Turkey and India-Pakistan.

If the aim for 'success' is both improved disaster-related activities and increased diplomatic activities, then the strong potential for failure by linking disaster-related activities and diplomacy is foreseeable, irrespective of the hazard's time and space scales. Rather than linking them, policy makers might wish to pursue different pathways to achieve separate successes for disaster-related activities and for diplomacy.

Disaster risk reduction and disaster response being political processes means that they must be linked to politics, but that does not mean that they must necessarily be linked to diplomacy beyond the disaster-related activities. The technical and social components of disaster response and disaster risk reduction, the links between the technical and social components, and numerous success stories are well-established (Hewitt, 1983; Lewis, 1999; Wisner et al., 2004, 2012). The work of organisations such as CDEMA, ECHO, SPC SOPAC, and UNISDR, described in section 3, provides an entry point to disaster-related activities at multiple governance scales. If intentionality is to succeed at vulnerability reduction and humanitarian aid, then it is foreseeable that seeking wider diplomatic outcomes from disaster-related activities is not likely to be the most effective means.

Similarly, if intentionality is to achieve more diplomacy-related successes, then it is foreseeable that focusing on disaster-related activities is not likely to be the most effective means. In India and Pakistan, when the 2001 earthquake jump-started diplomacy, the result was that the process was soon worse off than before the earthquake. Then, in 2005, both countries exercised caution by not linking disaster response and diplomacy for Kashmir. Conversely, film diplomacy through Bollywood has had substantive success in disseminating India's culture, political views, and values outside the country, creating a generally positive image (Roy, 2012). In sports diplomacy, the marriage in 2010 of India's tennis star Sania Mirza to Pakistan's former cricket captain Shoaib Malik was represented in the media as forging a link of India-Pakistan friendship.

No statement is made that film diplomacy, sports diplomacy, or celebrity diplomacy is the most effective for political diplomacy. The studies available are limited, but they do point to some level of achievement (Cooper, 2008; Roy, 2012), although it is hard to know how much might be wishful thinking or expectations of success—exactly as with much media coverage of disaster diplomacy. The media's, and even the populace's, objectives might not necessarily match with the objectives of the people and institutions with governing power, especially in terms of disaster-related activities, diplomacy, and their links.

The evidence presented above, from the theorising to the case studies, demonstrates that not all parties necessarily want disaster-related activities or diplomacy to succeed. As such, no assumption should be made regarding their intentionality with respect to disaster diplomacy and there is no inherent reason why disaster diplomacy should be expected to succeed. In terms of disaster risk reduction not necessarily being a high political priority, the legislation from Mongolia, South Africa, and the U.S.A., noted in section 3, indicates that even with good practice case studies, other political considerations can preclude the legislation achieving its disaster-related goals on its own. In terms of disaster response not necessarily being a high political priority, perceived historic wrongs and domestic politics can outweigh accepting assistance, as shown in many instances (Nelson, 2010b) including Cuba and the U.S.A. refusing to accept aid from the other (Glantz, 2000; Kelman, 2007).

These examples are from governmental diplomacy. Others involved in diplomacy might be more inclined towards disaster diplomacy, as seen by the media and private citizens for Greece and Turkey.

Science diplomacy for disasters and disaster risk reduction refers to research and technical cooperation and exchange amongst states with some form of conflict, which could range from violent hostilities to major security concerns. This form of scientific and technical cooperation amongst individuals frequently occurs. British, American, and North Korean scientists have been collaborating to analyse the volcanology of Mount Paektu on the North Korea-China border (Stone, 2013). The Middle East has a long history of collaborating on seismic building codes. Substantive impacts on other diplomacy are not well-documented, as also described for the case studies in sections 5 and 6 in which science diplomacy is a core activity yet led to limited outcomes outside the scientific and technical cooperation.

Even for Cuba and the U.S.A., Glantz (2000) details the long history of Cuban and American weather and climate scientists collaborating while Fidel Castro led Cuba. These collaborations fed into disaster risk reduction and continued successfully, most likely because elements within the governments which would have opposed such work were not aware of it (Glantz, 2000), hence spillover into wider diplomacy was not forthcoming despite the disaster risk reduction successes. Glantz himself was involved in science diplomacy. He is an American who forged links with Cuban scientists during Fidel Castro's reign and with Soviet scientists during the Cold War.

Similar links have been built between American, British, and Iranian scientists. As with Glantz' (2000) description of Cuban-American science diplomacy, the Iran-U.S.A. and Iran-U.K. scientific collaborations, particularly for earthquake topics, might be permitted and successful because they are not overtly publicised and because any anti-collaboration echelons within governments were not fully aware of them—or chose to pretend not to be aware of them. Yet some collaboration might have been stymied through refusing visas to visit or through declining grant applications for joint ventures. Irrespective, any blocking or lack of awareness of scientific cooperation means that the scientific and technical collaboration would not have scope for influencing wider diplomatic processes. In particular, keeping the disaster-related work below the diplomatic radar means no prospects for disaster diplomacy—which might be positive for moving forward with disaster-related activities.

This complex web of interactions and deliberate non-interactions is to be expected given the complexities of diplomatic and disaster-related activities. Any linear analyses of connections, correlations, and causations are likely to have errors as will any expectations of direct cause-and-effect observations for disaster diplomacy. Consequently, a given starting point for exploring any disaster diplomacy case study does not necessarily convey a foreseeable and exact outcome. Even active disaster diplomacy to fulfil intentionality might fail. Given the importance of pre-existing conditions in directing whether and how disaster diplomacy becomes even a short-term catalyst, and given the multiple scales at which disaster-related and diplomatic activities operate, it is difficult to indicate precisely where disaster diplomacy analysis should begin in terms of space scale, time scale, governance level, and unit of analysis. How far back can one go in time and how wide can one cast the net spatially to determine pre-existing conditions?

Rather than seeking a clearly delineated indication of disaster diplomacy as being present or absent in a particular instance, the main implication for foreign policy is perhaps that disaster diplomacy is most adequately viewed as being a long-running process at multiple scales with multiple parties interacting in multiple ways. Disaster diplomacy is not a snapshot phenomenon that either succeeds or does not succeed. Disaster-related activities are indeed one influence amongst many or all forms of diplomacy. Diplomacy is indeed one political input amongst many or all forms of disaster-related activities. Other major influences include culture, education, entertainment, personalities, resources, science, sports, and trade.

The emphasis should be twofold. First, on choice. Intentionality exists and can be used to direct an outcome, provided that those with power examine and understand the likely consequences of possible pathways and choices. The second emphasis is thus foreseeability. Could those with power really understand the likely consequences of possible pathways and choices? How much time and other resources are required for a detailed understanding? In cases of disaster response, the time and other resources required to fully analyse disaster diplomacy pathways are usually not available. Intentionality, though, could be made clear even if foreseeability cannot be.

Determining intentions and whether or not those intentions should be fully and openly expressed, along with what is and is not foreseeable, could overcome the assumption of disaster-related activities as a quick fix to resolve conflict. As shown by the case studies, it is naïve to expect that decades or centuries of differences could be overcome overnight, simply because a tornado cut through a city (followed by disaster relief) or because a region-wide seismic-resistant building code was developed and promulgated (that is, disaster risk reduction). Even extensive media coverage at the time is not likely to overturn a lengthy history, especially as old patterns re-assert themselves when the media move on to other stories. In contrast, it is a truism that successfully dealing with both disaster and diplomacy are long-term processes, requiring thoughtful, careful steps, whilst ensuring that all key parties remain on board to support the long-term goals and to serve mutual interests—at least, in theory.

In practice, too much of diplomacy and disaster-related activities is conducted reactively with limited planning—which could mean that a disaster diplomacy case study might eventually succeed fully through luck. In particular, arguments for intentionality and foreseeability might not always withstand scrutiny from a foreign policy perspective.

In terms of intentionality, not everyone accepts the moral or legal obligation to enact disaster risk reduction or disaster response. Even where national legislation exists for disaster risk reduction—which can be in the form of specific laws or related legislation such as planning and building codes—disaster-related international obligations might not be covered. Responsibilities regarding multilateral disaster-related activities are extensively debated (e.g. Ferris, 2011), raising foreign policy difficulties with respect to intentionality. No claim can be made that foreign policy intends to save lives or to help others, meaning that intentionality regarding disaster diplomacy should never be assumed to exist, as discussed in section 4.3. Furthermore, diplomatic parties such as the media sometimes have a palpable effect on international disaster aid and the foreign policy links or lack thereof (Drury et al., 2005; Van Belle, 2003).

In terms of foreseeability, diplomacy is not a linear trajectory of decision-cause-effect. Circumstances and influences can be volatile while outcomes can depend on independent and dependent decisions by others individually and collectively, especially political leaders change. Greek-Turkish rapprochement would have been unlikely to proceed so swiftly without the foreign ministers' friendship. The rapprochement would not likely have entered the public eye if the media had not been so supportive of earthquake diplomacy. Without key elections in both Iran and the U.S.A. in 2004, more opportunity might have emerged to use the 2003 earthquake to cement continuing improvements in relations. Instead, the public spotlight on Iran-U.S.A. relations induced by the earthquake manoeuvred both governments into being keen to avoid being seen as giving in to their 'enemy'. Existing knowledge can give a solid indication of possible future pathways, but can rarely provide the exact consequences for a given foreign policy approach.

Foreseeability might be limited to laying out potential future pathways and outcomes, with some indication of each one's likelihood. It might not be fair to demand foreseeability with respect to disaster diplomacy—apart from making it clear that past experience displays limited long-term success for disaster diplomacy, mainly because those involved did not actively seek long-term success.

In any case, the lack of successful examples so far of new diplomacy based on only disaster-related activities does not preclude disaster diplomacy successes. Historical case studies not yet examined or future events might reveal clear-cut disaster diplomacy. For the moment, the evidence available shows that disaster diplomacy is not effective for supporting diplomacy. There are few consistent circumstances in which disaster diplomacy is bound to have some form of success, apart from the narrow band where (i) the main parties involved choose to actively seek it and (ii) substantive pre-existing conditions supporting its success are present. It seems likely that the presence of the second point would support the existence of the first point.

7.2 *Policy Maker Lessons*

Given the challenges articulated in section 7.1 and the view of disaster diplomacy as a process, what should a policy maker take from disaster diplomacy and apply to foreign policy? This section provides recommendations.

The baseline is complexity. Diplomacy is nefariously complex, as demonstrated by the various views of its definition, the diverse schools of thought surrounding it, and the differing views on overlaps, divergences, and synonymy amongst the words and phrases used in relation to it: diplomacy, peace, cooperation, rapprochement, reconciliation, conflict resolution, détente, and others. Disasters and disaster risk reduction, being fundamentally political, are also pernicious in their complexity, especially given how much technical and social knowledge exists yet is not applied. Combining disaster-related activities and diplomacy for disaster diplomacy layers complexity upon complexity.

Even a solidly formulated disaster diplomacy strategy involving all key parties can go awry due to the sudden death of a leader or a major terrorist attack by a fringe group. Indira Gandhi, Prime Minister of India, was assassinated by her bodyguards in 1984 while Zia-ul-Haq, President of Pakistan, died in a plane crash in 1988. What could either event have meant for any India-Pakistan disaster diplomacy, had a process been ongoing? Israeli-Palestinian peace was severely inhibited by the fallout from Israeli Prime Minister Yitzhak Rabin being shot and killed by an anti-peace Israeli (Newman, 1997). In 2015 in Turkey, bombs targeting peace rallies massacred dozens, specifically aiming to undermine peace processes. Intentionality is not necessarily in favour of diplomacy.

Ultimately, disaster-related activities are one influence on diplomacy amongst many other influences and vice versa. Diplomatic parties can determine for themselves, to some degree, how much they would like disaster-related activities to influence their diplomacy decisions. Thus far, the evidence basis is against disaster diplomacy succeeding on its own without wider contributions to diplomatic processes. Disaster diplomacy, or expectations thereof, can even set back diplomatic processes, as seen for the Greece-Turkey, India-Pakistan, disease diplomacy, and climate change diplomacy case studies.

It would be a grievous error to rely on disaster-related activities for diplomacy. This situation does not preclude actively using disaster diplomacy as part of wider diplomatic efforts, because the disaster diplomacy story is not yet over.

Much evidence remains to be collected, particularly in terms of long-term impacts within the disaster diplomacy sphere. As the immediate adrenaline-filled aftermath of a disaster is superseded by the day-to-day drudgery of survival by disaster-affected populations who cannot leave with the rescue crews or media, how long does the humanitarian aid stay in the recipients' minds? Will the washed-out government logo on a tattered tent bring fond memories of the help provided, creating a grateful population? Or would resentment grow that more was not done and that, after the initial aid splurge, little was forthcoming? If aid is perceived to be only a political tool or if the donor is too forthright that they wish to make friends and are using the assistance for that, could the admission breed an attitude of avoiding being led down a diplomatic path by a rich, privileged 'enemy'?

The individual links forged in disaster diplomacy processes can be important. The Greek and Turkish foreign ministers were strong drivers of Greek-Turkish diplomacy in the presence and absence of disasters, with their friendship being a tangible factor. Fidel Castro and many Cuban exiles in Florida were strong blockers of Cuba-U.S.A. diplomacy in the presence and absence of disasters. As alluded to for Iran-U.S.A. earthquake diplomacy and at the end of section 4, no one monitors how many rescuers stay in touch with those whom they rescued, nor the political positions the rescuers and rescuees adopt with regard to any political conflict that previously separated them. Little research covers the long-term impact on conflict of persistent memories of good deeds carried out by the enemy—or of good deeds attempted but being inadequate or of good deeds eschewed. These memories, good and bad, might fade for some people and endure for others.

Perhaps the most solid disaster diplomacy consequences are those that are least observable and least measurable. Consequently, no matter what the intentionality, they might not be foreseeable.

In summary, the main disaster diplomacy implications for foreign policy are:

- Do not rely on disaster-related activities for diplomacy. Even humanitarian relief can undermine or inhibit diplomacy.
- Disaster-related activities can be used actively to pursue diplomatic goals as long as those activities sit within wider diplomatic efforts and the diplomatic goals are sought for reasons other than disaster response or disaster risk reduction.
- Individuals can make a big difference with respect to disasters, diplomacy, and the connections, but individuals are not the only important factor.

7.3 *Future Research Agenda*

Despite the clear direction provided for policy makers, many research gaps remain. This section suggests priorities for a disaster diplomacy research agenda in four areas: (i) basic parameters of disaster diplomacy; (ii) science diplomacy for disasters and disaster risk reduction; (iii) meta-analyses of disaster diplomacy's potential impacts; and (iv) improved integration of research, policy, and practice.

Regarding basic parameters of disaster diplomacy, the call from Yim et al. (2009a, 291) remains apposite that 'disaster diplomacy lacks a formal definition of principles, metrics of success'. This statement is echoed by Streich and Mislan (2014), especially in pointing out inconsistencies and gaps in Kelman (2012) which ought to be redressed. While universal agreement might not be necessary or achievable regarding definitions, a basic and generally accepted description would be helpful regarding what disaster diplomacy is currently and could be. From that common baseline, parameters, metrics, and clearly delineated understandings of disaster diplomacy's successes, failures, and neutral impacts could emerge and help coherence for this research field. Limitations will always exist, so they need to be described openly.

The second area, science diplomacy, has not yet been covered extensively for disaster diplomacy although many scattered examples exist as described in section 7.1. Research questions include:

- Does this science diplomacy produce wider disaster diplomacy, such as for post-disaster response or wider diplomacy beyond disasters?
- Where political leaders were ostensibly unaware of the science diplomacy, could their ignorance have contributed to the science diplomacy's success, because politics interfered minimally with the science?

- Or would classified work within science diplomacy, which might be the most useful, be forbidden, meaning that politicians would have no need to be concerned?

These questions require further exploration, especially in conjunction with the rich literature already existing on science diplomacy of many forms (e.g. Davis and Patman, 2015).

With an improved understanding of what disaster diplomacy is, could be, and should be—including in its different forms, such as science diplomacy—the third area for a research agenda is meta-analyses of disaster diplomacy's implications, for foreign policy and beyond. Section 4.4 brought forward some ethical implications of disaster diplomacy in theory and practice. Research questions result. From the discussion on rescuer-rescuee relationships, is it ethical to consider the possibilities that rescuers will form bonds leading to peace and, therefore, to act on the basis of the low probability that diplomatic results will appear? What if rescuers and rescuees end up in conflict—or if failure to rescue tarnishes the would-be rescuers—destroying hopes of disaster diplomacy and perhaps even poisoning each other or one side to reconciliation? Are such considerations cleverly strategic, truly seeking long-term vulnerability reduction through disaster diplomacy? Or are they cheap, cynical manipulations of helping people in need for political purposes?

Ethical questions are relevant for determining who is aware of disaster diplomacy and if awareness makes any difference. As with the discussion above on science diplomacy, politicians and diplomats might not always know about all forms of disaster diplomacy or how striving for disaster diplomacy could potentially dictate its success or failure. What duty do disaster diplomacy researchers have to inform or not inform different groups regarding intentionality and foreseeability with respect to disaster diplomacy's foreign policy implications? In a disaster situation, should the implications be made explicit so that decision-makers can factor the issue into their deliberations on whether and how to offer or accept humanitarian aid? Should disaster diplomacy scientists accept any credit or blame for choices made and the results? This part of the disaster diplomacy research agenda would cover the impacts and implications of the disaster diplomacy research process and results on diplomacy processes and diplomatic decision-making.

The fourth and final area for further research is reiterating calls in the literature for improved connections amongst disaster diplomacy research, policy, and practice. Yim et al. (2009a, 291) call for 'a strategy for integration into formal diplomatic efforts, and a dedicated training program for humanitarian agents planning to engage in this form of diplomacy'. Their suggestions remain unfulfilled, emphasised by Streich and Mislan (2014, p. 85) explaining that 'This field has room to grow into a pillar of practical and theory-relevant research' and 'calling for greater multimethod empirical work'. Such work would inform policy makers and practitioners regarding what they should seek and how they should respond to instances of potential disaster diplomacy.

8 Epilogue: The Future of Disaster Diplomacy Influencing Foreign Policy

8.1 *Bringing Together Aceh and Sri Lanka*

With the understanding of disaster diplomacy and of the circumstances under which success could be actively pursued (or not) and occurs (or does not occur), the case study from section 1 of the 26 December 2004 earthquake and tsunami can be explained (using also analysis from Enia, 2008; Gaillard et al., 2008; Kelman, 2012; and Le Billon and Waizenegger, 2007). In the disaster's aftermath, why did Aceh reach a peace deal whereas Sri Lanka did not? The key is the explanation of disaster diplomacy's impact that disaster-related activities can sometimes catalyse diplomacy in the short-term if there are pre-existing conditions, but disaster-related activities thus far have not been shown to be able to create new peace which lasts over the long-term.

In Sri Lanka, few of the power brokers involved in the conflict had much impetus towards peace. Many outside the northern and eastern parts of the island opposed any attempts to deal with the Tamil de facto government because they felt that it would legitimise terrorism, as subsequently backed up by the Supreme Court and the Sri Lankan electorate, described in section 1. Meanwhile, on the side of those fighting the Sri Lankan government, many leaders did not have an incentive for peace. They were comfortable in the power and control they held in the territory which they effectively governed, they were supported by a worldwide diaspora, and they were not expecting a fair deal for themselves in any peace talks. The lack of pre-existing conditions in which a peace deal in Sri Lanka could be reached and the lack of impetus towards peace from the parties involved meant that the situation ramped up towards further violence, reached it, and then a brutal military approach eventually ended the conflict.

In Sri Lanka, intentionality from many of the parties involved favoured violence, no matter what the consequences were for disaster response. They succeeded in achieving their intentions, precluding hope for disaster diplomacy. Foreseeability dictates that people suffering due to the tsunami and the conflict would be expected—which happened. Following the end of the military campaign, the country was able to move forward with post-conflict, post-tsunami reconstruction with no need for disaster diplomacy because the war was over. No circumstances could have led to disaster diplomacy success, because the parties involved did not seek disaster diplomacy success.

Meanwhile, in Aceh, there was no doubt that the disaster created political space in which the diplomacy had an opportunity to succeed. It was as clear that the disaster did not create the peace deal, because Gaillard et al. (2008) report that the talks which led to the final peace accord had started secretly on 24 December 2004, just 48 hours before the devastation.

Those talks emerged from previous months of back-and-forth diplomacy between the parties who wanted peace and who had the power to achieve it. In October 2004, Susilo Bambang Yudhoyono was elected President of Indonesia with Y. Kalla as Vice President. In previous months, Yalla had established contact with Acehnese separatist negotiators to set the stage for talks. Following the election, Yalla's efforts led to a secret agreement between the Indonesian government and Acehnese separatists which collapsed when it was publicly revealed. Then, in November 2004, Yudhoyono visited Aceh to describe his willingness to continue seeking peace. The Acehnese were interested, leading to the opening of negotiations on 24 December.

When the disaster struck on 26 December, the connections between the parties and the desire for diplomacy had already been established, representing the pre-existing conditions. The disaster could be used as a catalyst for diplomacy if those involved wished to pursue that pathway. They did, with the parties displaying intentionality regarding the success of the diplomacy and applying foreseeability to determine how to make best use of the opportunity available. The circumstances which could lead to disaster diplomacy success existed, in terms of ending the conflict and reconstructing post-disaster and post-conflict, because the parties sought such disaster diplomacy success based on their mutual interests in the process.

In Aceh, the parties involved seized the 'opportunity' of the tsunami and earthquake disaster to end the war. Those fighting had pre-existing reasons for wanting peace and were seeking excuses for it, which they found in the disaster. Both intentionality and foreseeability were present regarding disaster diplomacy, so the parties achieved their aim. Conversely, in Sri Lanka, they seized the tsunami disaster 'opportunity' to exacerbate the conflict. Those fighting had pre-existing reasons for wanting conflict and were seeking excuses for it, which they found in the disaster. Both intentionality and foreseeability were present, but for conflict rather than for peace.

In both islands, the parties with the power already knew what disaster diplomacy 'success' meant for them, they pursued their preferred disaster diplomacy outcome, and they achieved that preferred outcome. In one location, Aceh, the consequence was disaster as a catalyst for diplomacy, not a direct and causal link from disaster to diplomacy, but a modicum of disaster diplomacy success in that peace was reached, permitting post-earthquake, post-tsunami, post-conflict reconstruction. In the other location, Sri Lanka, the parties with the power also already knew what disaster diplomacy 'success' would mean for them, so they pursued their preferred disaster diplomacy outcome, and they achieved that outcome. Disaster diplomacy was an abject failure.

The 26 December 2004 tsunami as a disaster diplomacy case study indicates that success is achievable when directly pursued—but the meaning of disaster diplomacy's success varies according to the perspective adopted.

8.2 *The Meaning of Disaster Diplomacy for Foreign Policy*

To return to the main research question of this paper, under what circumstances could disaster diplomacy be actively made to succeed or not succeed? 26 December 2004 illustrates the overarching answer, further corroborated by the old and new case studies presented here and in the wider literature. The circumstances are that those with the power to make disaster diplomacy succeed or fail need to decide what they want and then use their power to achieve their goal. If parties with power align in their goals, then their common goal will likely succeed, whether that goal is peace, conflict, or neither. If parties with power do not align in their goals, then it is much easier to continue conflict than to achieve peace. Either way, disaster diplomacy as an active process is not the fundamental driver of peace or conflict.

This paper has explored the state-of-the-art in 'disaster diplomacy' research while indicating its foreign policy implications. The material summarises the current view of disaster diplomacy and some previous case studies which led to this view, alongside the poignant critiques of the earlier work, especially the criticisms noting how some past work did not fully integrate previous literature. Two new case studies are provided—disease diplomacy and climate change diplomacy—which are used to further interpret the theoretical understanding of disaster diplomacy. Direct recommendations for policy makers are given followed by a research agenda to plug some of the remaining gaps.

The importance in learning more about the research, policy, and practice of disaster diplomacy is in overcoming the assumption and expectation of many pursuing disaster-related activities that a humanitarian imperative must bring parties together, irrespective of the state of conflict of those parties. Desperate need or the desire to assist others does not necessarily translate into reconciliation unless a non-disaster-related baseline exists in conjunction with a determination to pursue reconciliation for non-disaster-related reasons. The reality is that, in political realms, considerations can be prioritised other than providing as much assistance as possible to those in need as soon as possible—considerations which then translate into diplomatic activities or lack thereof.

For foreign policy, the consequence is that disaster-related activities can sometimes appear to drive activities and decisions, but the influence so far has been shown to be superficial and not long-lasting. For actively directing foreign policy, disaster-related activities cannot be relied on to forge substantial connections or to make fundamental progress—but disaster-related activities can be applied as a reason for driving forward policy goals which already exist for non-disaster-related reasons.

References

Acuto, M. (ed.) 2014. *Negotiating Relief: The Dialectics of Humanitarian Space*. London: Hurst Publishers.

Aitsi-Selmi, A., S. Egawa, H. Sasaki, C. Wannous, and V. Murray. 2015. The Sendai Framework for Disaster Risk Reduction: Renewing the Global Commitment to People's Resilience, Health, and Well-being. *International Journal of Disaster Risk Science*, 6(2), 164–76. DOI 10.1007/s13753-015-0050-9.

Aldrich, D.P. 2012. *Building Resilience: Social Capital in Post-Disaster Recovery*. Chicago: University of Chicago Press.

Alexander, D.E. 2007. Misconception as a barrier to teaching about disasters. *Prehospital and Disaster Medicine*, 22(2), 95–103.

Anderson, M.B. 1999. *Do No Harm: How Aid can Support Peace–or War*. London: Lynne Rienner.

Baldacchino, G. and D. Milne (eds.) 2009. *The Case for Non-Sovereignty: Lessons from Sub-National Island Jurisdictions*. London: Taylor and Francis.

Bar-Dayan, Y., D. Mankuta, Y. Wolf, Y. Levy, M. VanRooyen, P. Beard, A. Finestone, C. Gruzman, P. Benedek, and G. Martonovits. 2000. An Earthquake Disaster in Turkey: An Overview of the Experience of the Israeli Defence Forces Field Hospital in Adapazari. *Disasters*, 24(3), 262–70. DOI 10.1111/1467-7717.00147.

Barry, M. 2006. Slaying Little Dragons: Lessons From the Dracunculiasis Eradication Program. *American Journal of Tropical Medicine and Hygiene*, 75(1), 1–2.

Beyrer, C., J.C. Villar, V. Suwanvanichkij, S. Singh, S.D. Baral, and E.J. Mills. 2007. Neglected diseases, civil conflicts, and the right to health. *The Lancet*, 370, 619–27.

Bhutto, A.W., A.A. Bazmi, and G. Zahedi. 2014. Greener energy: Issues and challenges for Pakistan—Solar energy prospective. *Renewable and Sustainable Energy Reviews*, 16, 2762–80. DOI 10.1016/j.rser.2012.02.043.

Bishop, P., D. Sanderson, J. Hansom, and N. Chaimanee. 2005. Age-dating of tsunami deposits: lessons from the 26 December 2004 tsunami in Thailand. *The Geographical Journal*, 171(4), 379–84. DOI 10.1111/j.1475-4959.2005.00175_4.x.

Biswas, G., D.P. Sankara, J. Agua-Agum, and A. Maiga. 2013. Dracunculiasis (guinea worm disease): Eradication without a drug or a vaccine. *Philosophical Transactions of the Royal Society B*, 68, 20120146. DOI dx.doi.org/10.1098/rstb.2012.0146.

Blondet, M., G. Villa-Garcia, S. Brzev, and Á. Rubiños. 2011. Earthquake-resistant construction of adobe buildings: A tutorial. EERI (Earthquake Engineering Research Institute), Oakland, California.

Boas, I. 2015. *Climate Migration and Security: Securitisation as a Strategy in Climate Change Politics*. Abingdon: Routledge.

Bohlen, A. 2015. Iran: An Opening for Diplomacy? *Survival: Global Politics and Strategy*, 57(5), 59–66.

Breman, J.G. and I. Arita. 1980. The confirmation and maintenance of smallpox eradication. *The New England Journal of Medicine*, 303(22), 1263–73.

Bronen, R. and F.S. Chapin III. 2013. Adaptive governance and institutional strategies for climate-induced community relocations in Alaska. *PNAS*, 110(23), 9320–25. DOI 10.1073/pnas.1210508110.

Bruintjes, R.T. 1999. A Review of Cloud Seeding Experiments to Enhance Precipitation and Some New Prospects. *Bulletin of the American Meteorological Society*, 80, 805–20. DOI dx.doi.org/10.1175/1520-0477(1999)080<0805:AROCSE>2.0.CO;2.

Bull, H. 1977. *The Anarchical Society: A Study of Order in World Politics*. New York: Columbia University Press.

Burns, T.R. and H. Flam. 1987. *The Shaping of Social Organization: Social Rule System Theory with Applications*. London: Sage.

Bush, K. 2004. Commodification, Compartmentalization, and Militarization of Peacebuilding. In T. Keating and A. Knight (eds.), *Building Sustainable Peace*, Edmonton, Alberta: University of Alberta Press, pp. 23–46.

Butler, R.A. and W.F. Laurance. 2008. New strategies for conserving tropical forests. *Trends in Ecology & Evolution*, 23(9), 469–72. DOI 10.1016/j.tree.2008.05.006.

Cable, J. 1971. *Gunboat Diplomacy*. New York: Praeger.

Carlile, J.A., K. Mauseth, N.E. Clark, J.L. Cruz, J.W. Thoburn. 2015. Local Volunteerism and Resilience Following Large-Scale Disaster: Outcomes for Health Support Team Volunteers in Haiti. *International Journal of Disaster Risk Science*, 5(3), 206–13. DOI 10.1007/s13753-014-0028-z.

Casey, C.G., J.K. Iskander, M.H. Roper, E.E. Mast, X.-J. Wen, T.J. Török, L.E. Chapman, D.L. Swerdlow, J. Morgan, J.D. Heffelfinger, C. Vitek, S.E. Reef, L.M. Hasbrouck, I. Damon, L. Neff, C. Vellozzi, M. McCauley, R.A. Strikas, G. Mootrey. 2005. Adverse Events Associated With Smallpox Vaccination in the United States, January–October 2003. *JAMA*, 294(21), 2734–43. DOI 10.1001/jama.294.21.2734.

Cash, R.A., S.R. Halder, M. Husain, Md.S. Islam, F.H. Mallick, M.A. May, M. Rahman, and M.A. Rahman. 2013. Reducing the health effect of natural hazards in Bangladesh. *The Lancet*, 382(9910), 2094–2103. DOI 10.1016/S0140-6736(13)61948-0.

Chen, L.-C., Y.-C. Liu, and K.-C. Chan. 2006. Integrated Community-Based Disaster Management Program in Taiwan: A Case Study of Shang-An Village. *Natural Hazards*, 37(1), 209–23. DOI 10.1007/s11069-005-4669-5.

Coburn, A.W. and R.J.S Spence. 2002. *Earthquake Protection*. London: John Wiley & Sons.

Coch, N.K. 1995. *Geohazards: Natural and Human*. New Jersey: Prentice-Hall.

Comfort, L. 2000. Disaster: agent of diplomacy or change in international affairs? *Cambridge Review of International Affairs*, XIV(1), 277–94.

Connell, J. 1997. *Papua New Guinea: The Struggle for Development*. London: Routledge.

Cooper, A.F. 2008. *Celebrity Diplomacy*. Boulder: Paradigm.

Cooper, B. 2006. Poxy models and rash decisions. *PNAS*, 103(33), 12221–22. DOI 10.1073/pnas.0605502103.

Cyranoski, D. 2005. Get off the beach—Now! *Nature*, 433, 354. DOI 10.1038/433354a.

Dang, H.H., A. Michaelowa, and D.D. Tuan. 2003. Synergy of adaptation and mitigation strategies in the context of sustainable development: The case of Vietnam. *Climate Policy*, 3S1, S81–S96. DOI 10.1016/j.clipol.2003.10.006.

Davidson, W.D. and J.V. Montville. 1981. Foreign Policy According to Freud. *Foreign Affairs*, Winter 1981–82, 145–57.

Davis, L.S. and R.G. Patman. 2015. *Science Diplomacy: New Day or False Dawn?* Singapore: World Scientific Publishing.

De Boer, J.Z. and D.T. Sanders 2004. *Volcanoes in Human History: The Far-Reaching Effects of Major Eruptions*. Princeton, NJ: Princeton University Press.

———. 2005. *Earthquakes in Human History: The Far-Reaching Effects of Seismic Disruptions*. Princeton, NJ: Princeton University Press.

Desinventar. 2015. Information from http://www.desinventar.org Last accessed 3 August 2015.

Diamond, L. and J. McDonald. 1993. *Multi-Track Diplomacy: A Systems Approach to Peace*. Washington, D.C.: Institute for Multi-Track Diplomacy.

Domínguez, J.I. 1997. U.S.-Cuban Relations: From the Cold War to the Colder War. *Journal of Interamerican Studies and World Affairs*, 39(3), 49–75. DOI 10.1111/j.1548-2456.1997.tb00039.x.

Dove, M.R. 1998. Local dimensions of 'global' environmental debates. In A. Kalland and G. Persoon (eds.), *Environmental Movements in Asia*, Richmond, Surrey: Curzon Press: 44–64.

Dove, M.R. and M.H. Khan. 1995. Competing constructions of calamity: the April 1991 Bangladesh cyclone. *Population and Environment*, 16(5), 445–71. DOI 10.1007/BF02209425.

Draper, G., T. Vincent, and M.E. Kroll. 2005. Childhood Cancer in Relation to Distance from High Voltage Power Lines in England and Wales: A Case-control Study. *BMJ*, 330(7503), 1290. DOI 10.1136/bmj.330.7503.1290.

Drury, A.C. and R.S. Olson. 1998. Disasters and political unrest: an empirical investigation. *Journal of Contingencies and Crisis Management*, 6(3), 153–61. DOI 10.1111/1468-5973.00084.

Drury, A.C., R.S. Olson, and D.A. Van Belle. 2005. The Politics of Humanitarian Aid: U.S. Foreign Disaster Assistance, 1964–1995. *Journal of Politics*, 67(2), 454–73 DOI 10.1111/j.1468-2508.2005.00324.x.

Durrheim, D.N. and M. Dahl-Regis. 2014. The Ethical Imperative to Eradicate Measles. *Journal of Clinical Research & Bioethics*, 5(3), 1–3. DOI 10.4172/2155-9627.1000183.

Dybas, C.L. 2005. Native lore tells tale. *Oceanography*, 18(4), 12. DOI 10.5670/oceanog.2005.17.

EM-DAT. 2015. Information from http://www.emdat.be. Last accessed 3 August 2015.

Enarson, E. and B.H. Morrow (eds.) 1998. *The Gendered Terrain of Disaster: Through Women's Eyes*. CT: Greenwood Publications.

Enia, J. 2008. Peace in its Wake? The 2004 Tsunami and internal conflict in Indonesia and Sri Lanka. *Journal of Public and International Affairs*, 19, 7–27.

Felli, R. and N. Castree. 2012. Neoliberalising adaptation to environmental change: foresight or foreclosure? *Environment and Planning A*, 44, 1–4. DOI 10.1068/a44680.

Fenner, F. 1982. Global Eradication of Smallpox. *Clinical Infectious Diseases*, 4(5), 916–30. DOI 10.1093/clinids/4.5.916.

Ferguson, N.M., M.J. Keeling, W.J. Edmunds, R. Gani, B.T. Grenfell, R.M. Anderson, and S. Leach. 2003. Planning for smallpox outbreaks. *Nature*, 425, 681–85. DOI 10.1038/nature02007.

Ferris, E.G. 2011. *The Politics of Protection: The Limits of Humanitarian Action*. Washington DC: Brookings Institute.

Fisher, A. 2013. *Collaborative Public Diplomacy: How Transnational Networks Influenced American Studies in Europe*. New York: Palgrave MacMillan.

Foege, W.H. 1982. The Global Elimination of Measles. *Public Health Reports*, 97(5), 402–05.

Forced Migration Review. 2008. *Climate change and displacement*, 31(October), 1–80.

Gaillard J.C., J.R.D. Cadag, M. Fellizar-Cagay, A. Francisco, and A. Glipo. 2011. *Participatory Three-Dimensional Mapping for Reducing the Risk of Disasters in Irosin*, Philippines. Paris: Comité Catholique contre la Faim et pour le Développement.

Gaillard, J.-C., E. Clavé, and I. Kelman. 2008. Wave of peace? Tsunami disaster diplomacy in Aceh, Indonesia. *Geoforum*, 39(1), 511–26. DOI 10.1016/j.geoforum.2007.10.010.

Gaillard, J.C., E. Clavé, O. Vibert, D. Azhari, J.-C. Denain, Y. Efendi, D. Grancher, C.C. Liamzon, D.S.R. Sari, and R. Setiawan. 2008. Ethnic groups' response to the

26 December 2004 earthquake and tsunami in Aceh, Indonesia. *Natural Hazards*, 47(1), 17–38. DOI 10.1007/s11069-007-9193-3.

Garber, R. 2002. Health as a Bridge for Peace: Theory, Practice and Prognosis—Reflections of a Practitioner. *Journal of Peacebuilding & Development*, 1(1), 69–84. DOI 10.1080/15423166.2002.827416170519.

Garon, J.R. and W.A. Orenstein. 2015. Overcoming barriers to polio eradication in conflict areas. *The Lancet Infectious Diseases*, 15, 1122–24. DOI dx.doi.org/10.1016/S1473-3099(15)00008-0.

Gifis, S. 1991. *Law Dictionary*, 3rd edition. New York: Barron's Educational Series.

Gladwell, M. 2000. *The Tipping Point: How Little Things Can Make a Big Difference*. New York: Little, Brown and Company.

Glantz, M.H. 1976. *The Politics of Natural Disaster: The Case of the Sahel Drought*. New York: Praeger.

———. 1994a. Creeping environmental problems. *The World & I*, June, 218–25.

———. 1994b. Creeping environmental phenomena: Are societies equipped to deal with them? In M.H. Glantz (ed.), *Creeping Environmental Phenomena and Societal Responses to Them, Proceedings of Workshop* held 7–10 February 1994 in Boulder, Colorado. Boulder: NCAR/ESIG, 1–10.

——— (ed.) 1999. *Creeping Environmental Problems and Sustainable Development in the Aral Sea Basin*. Cambridge: Cambridge University Press.

———. 2000. Climate-related disaster diplomacy: a US–Cuban case study. Cambridge *Review of International Affairs*, XIV(1), 233–253. DOI 10.1080/09557570008400340.

———. 2003. *Climate Affairs: A Primer*. Washington, DC: Island Press.

Glantz, M.H. and H. Cullen. 2003. Zimbabwe's Food Crisis. *Environment*, 45(1), 9–11.

Gostin, L.O. 2014. Global Polio Eradication: Espionage, Disinformation, and the Politics of Vaccination. *The Milbank Quarterly*, 92(3), 413–17. DOI 10.1111/1468-0009.12065.

Gregg, C.E., B.F. Houghton, D. Paton, R. Lachman, J. Lachman, D.M. Johnston, D.M., and S. Wongbusarakum. 2006. Natural warning signs of tsunamis: Human sensory experience and response to the 2004 Great Sumatra earthquake and tsunami in Thailand. *Earthquake Spectra*, 22(S3), S671-S691. DOI http://dx.doi.org/10.1193/1.2206791.

Hartmann, B. 2010. Rethinking climate refugees and climate conflict: rhetoric, reality and the politics of policy discourse. *Journal of International Development*, 22, 233–46. DOI 10.1002/jid.1676.

HDR. 2014. *2014 Human Development Report—Sustaining Human Progress: Reducing Vulnerabilities and Building Resilience*. New York: UNDP (United Nations Development Programme).

Hewitt, K. (ed.) 1983. *Interpretations of Calamity from the Viewpoint of Human Ecology*. Boston: Allen & Unwin.

Hollis, S. 2015. *The Role of Regional Organizations in Disaster Risk Management: A Strategy*. New York: Palgrave Macmillan.

Holloway, A. 2000. Drought emergency, yes ... drought disaster, no: Southern Africa 1991–93. *Cambridge Review of International Affairs*, XIV(1), 254–76. DOI 10.1080/09557570008400341.

Hopkins, D.R., J.P. Koplan, A.R. Hinman, and J.M. Lane. 1982. The Case For Global Measles Eradication. *The Lancet*, 319(8286), 1396–98. DOI 10.1016/S0140-6736(82)92510-7.

Hopkins, D.R., E. Ruiz-Tiben, T.K. Ruebush, N. Diallo, A. Agle, and P.C. Withers Jr. 2000. Dracunculiasis Eradication: Delayed, Not Denied. *American Journal Of Tropical Medicine and Hygiene*, 62(2), 163–68.

Hotez, P.J. 2001a. Vaccine Diplomacy. *Foreign Policy*, May/June, 68–69.

———. 2001b. Vaccines as Instruments of Foreign Policy. *EMBO Reports*, 2(10), 862–68. DOI 10.1093/embo-reports/kve215.

———. 2004. The Promise of Medical Science and Biotechnology for North Korea and the Relevance of U.S. 'Vaccine Diplomacy'. *Korea Society Quarterly*, 13(4), 15–18.

———. 2010. Peace Through Vaccine Diplomacy. *Science*, 327(5971), 1301. DOI 10.1126/science.1189028.

Hotez, P.J. and T.G. Thompson. 2009. Waging Peace through Neglected Tropical Disease Control: A US Foreign Policy for the Bottom Billion. *PLoS Neglected Tropical Diseases*, 3(1), e346. DOI 10.1371/journal.pntd.0000346.

Howard-Hassmann, R.E. 2010. Mugabe's Zimbabwe, 2000–2009: Massive Human Rights Violations and the Failure to Protect. *Human Rights Quarterly*, 32(4), 898–920. DOI 10.1353/hrq.2010.0030.

Hutchinson, E. 2014. A global politics of pity? Disaster imagery and emotional construction of solidarity after the 2004 Asian Tsunami. *International Political Sociology*, 8(1), 1–19. DOI 10.1111/ips.12037.

IFRC. 2009. *Humanitarian Diplomacy Policy*. Geneva: IFRC (International Federation of Red Cross and Red Crescent Societies).

———. 2014. *World Disasters Report 2014: Focus on culture and risk*. Geneva: International Federation of Red Cross and Red Crescent Societies.

IPCC. 2013–2014. *IPCC Fifth Assessment Report*. Geneva: IPCC (Intergovernmental Panel on Climate Change).

Jackson, J. 2001. Living with earthquakes: know your faults. *Journal of Earthquake Engineering*, 5(special issue 1), 5–123. DOI 10.1080/13632460109350530.

James, R. 2005. *Marine Biogeochemical Cycles*, 2nd edition. Amsterdam: Elsevier.

Jeggle, T. 2013. *Strategy Report on Disaster Risk Management, Reduction and Response in Mongolia*. For the UNISDR/North-East Asia Office, Inchon, Republic of Korea, and The Office of the United Nations Resident Coordinator in Mongolia Ulaanbaatar, Mongolia.

Kamalipour, Y.R. and N. Snow (eds.) 2004. *War, Media, and Propaganda: A Global Perspective*. Oxford: Rowman & Littlefield.

Kelly, H. 2011. The classical definition of a pandemic is not elusive. *Bulletin of the World Health Organization*, 89, 540–41. DOI 10.2471/BLT.11.088815.

Kelman, I. 2006. Warning for the 26 December 2004 Tsunamis. *Disaster Prevention and Management*, 15(1), 178–89. DOI 10.1108/09653560610654329.

———. 2007. Hurricane Katrina Disaster Diplomacy. *Disasters*, 31(3), 288–309. DOI 10.1111/j.0361-3666.2007.01010.x.

———. 2012. *Disaster Diplomacy: How Disasters Affect Peace and Conflict*. Routledge, Abingdon, Oxfordshire, U.K.

Kelman, I., M. Davies, T. Mitchell, I. Orr, and B. Conrich. 2006. Island Disaster Para-Diplomacy in the Commonwealth. *The Round Table: The Commonwealth Journal of International Affairs*, 95(386), 561–74. DOI 10.1080/00358530600929925.

Kelman, I., J.C. Gaillard, and J. Mercer. 2015. Climate Change's Role in Disaster Risk Reduction's Future: Beyond Vulnerability and Resilience. *International Journal of Disaster Risk Science*, 6(1), 21–27. DOI 10.1007/s13753-015-0038-5.

Kelman, I. and T. Koukis (eds.) 2000. Disaster Diplomacy. *Section in Cambridge Review of International Affairs*, 14(1), 214–94. DOI 10.1080/09557570008400338.

Ker-Lindsay, J. 2000. Greek–Turkish rapprochement: the impact of 'disaster diplomacy'? *Cambridge Review of International Affairs*, XIV(1), 215–32. DOI 10.1080/09557570008400339.

———. 2007. *Crisis and Conciliation: A Year of Rapprochement between Greece and Turkey*. London: IB Tauris.

Kevany, S. 2014. Global Health Diplomacy, 'Smart Power', and the New World Order. *Global Public Health*, 9(7), 787–807. DOI dx.doi.org/10.1080/17441692.2014.921219.

Kickbusch, I. 2011. Global health diplomacy: how foreign policy can influence health. *BMJ*, 342, d3154. DOI dx.doi.org/10.1136/bmj.d3154.

Krebs, D.R. 2003. *When Violence Erupts: A Survival Guide for Emergency Responders*. Burlington, MA: Jones and Bartlett Publishers.

Klinenberg, E. 2002. *Heat Wave: A Social Autopsy of Disaster in Chicago*. Chicago: University of Chicago Press.

Knutson, T.R., J.L. McBride, J. Chan, K. Emanuel, G. Holland, C. Landsea, I. Held, J.P. Kossin, A.K. Srivastava, and M. Sugi. 2010. Tropical cyclones and climate change. *Nature Geoscience*, 3, 157–263. DOI 10.1038/ngeo779.

Korauaba, T. 2015. Kiribati. *The Contemporary Pacific*, 27(1), 232–38. DOI 10.1353/cp.2015.0025.

Krüger, F., G. Bankoff, T. Cannon, B. Orlowski, and E.L. Schipper (eds.) 2015. *Cultures and Disasters: Understanding Cultural Framings in Disaster Risk Reduction*. Abingdon, Oxfordshire: Routledge.

Kunreuther, H.C. and G.F. White. 1994. The Role of the National Flood Insurance Program in Reducing Losses and Promoting Wise Use of Floodplains. *Journal of Contemporary Water Research and Education*, 95(1), 31–35.

Kurbalija, J. and V. Katrandjiev (eds.) 2006. *Multistakeholder Diplomacy—Challenges and Opportunities*. Msida, Malta: DiploFoundation.

Kutney, G. 2014. *Carbon Politics and the Failure of the Kyoto Protocol*. Abingdon: Routledge.

La Red, OSSO, and ISDR. 2002. *Comparative analysis of disaster databases: Final Report*. La Red and OSSO for UNDP and ISDR, Panama City and Geneva.

Lay, T., H. Kanamori, C.J. Ammon, M. Nettles, S.N. Ward, R.C. Aster, S.L. Beck, S.L. Bilek, M.R. Brudzinski, R. Butler, H.R. DeShon, G. Ekström, K. Satake, and S. Sipkin. 2005. The Great Sumatra-Andaman Earthquake of 26 December 2004. *Science*, 308(5725), 1127–33. DOI 10.1126/science.1112250.

Le Billon, P. and A. Waizenegger. 2007. Peace in the wake of disaster? Secessionist conflicts and the 2004 Indian Ocean tsunami. *Transactions of the Institute of British Geographers*, 32(3), 411–27. DOI 10.1111/j.1475-5661.2007.00257.x.

LeoGrande, W.M. 2008/2009. Engaging Cuba: A Roadmap. *World Policy Journal*, 25(4), 87–99. DOI 10.1162/wopj.2009.25.4.87.

Levy, M. and M. Salvadori. 1995. *Why the Earth Quakes: The Story of Earthquakes and Volcanoes*. U.S.A.: W.W. Norton & Company.

Lewis, J. 1984. Environmental Interpretations of Natural Disaster Mitigation: The Crucial Need. *The Environmentalist*, 4, 177–80.

———. 1999. *Development in Disaster-prone Places: Studies of Vulnerability*. London: Intermediate Technology Publications.

———. 2003. Housing construction in earthquake-prone places: perspectives, priorities and projections for development. *Australian Journal of Emergency Management*, 18(2), 35–44.

Licina, M.A.J.D. 2011. Disaster Preparedness—Formalizing a Comparative Advantage for the Department of Defense in U.S. Global Health and Foreign Policy. *Military Medicine*, 176(11), 1207–11.

Mariner, J.C., J.A. House, C.A. Mebus, A.E. Sollod, D. Chibeu, B.A. Jones, P.L. Roeder, B. Admassu, and G.G.M. van 't Klooster. 2012. Rinderpest Eradication: Appropriate Technology and Social Innovations. *Science*, 337, 1309–12. DOI 10.1126/science.1223805.

Marulanda, M.C., O.D. Cardona, and A.H. Barbat. 2010. Revealing the socioeconomic impact of small disasters in Colombia using the DesInventar database. *Disasters*, 34(2), 552–70. DOI 10.1111/j.0361-3666.2009.01143.x.

Mavrogenis, S. and I. Kelman. 2013. Perceptions of Greece-Turkey Disaster Diplomacy: Europeanization and the Underdog Culture. *Balkanistica*, 26, 73–104.

McGuire, B. 2010. Potential for a hazardous geospheric response to projected future climate changes. *Philosophical Transactions of the Royal Society A*, 368, 2317–45. doi:10.1098/rsta.2010.0080.

Minear, L. and H. Smith (eds.) 2007. *Humanitarian diplomacy: Practitioners and their craft*. Tokyo: United Nations University Press.

Mohapatra, M., B. Geetha, S. Balachandran, and L.S. Rathore. 2015. On the Tropical Cyclone Activity and Associated Environmental Features over North Indian Ocean in the Context of Climate Change. *Journal of Climate Change*, 1(1,2), 1–26. DOI 10.3233/JCC-150001.

Morens, D.M., E.C. Holmes, A.S. Davis, and J.K. Taubenberger. 2011. Global Rinderpest Eradication: Lessons Learned and Why Humans Should Celebrate Too. *The Journal of Infectious Diseases*, 204(4), 502–05. DOI 10.1093/infdis/jir327.

Mulargia, F. and A. Bizzarri. 2014. Anthropogenic Triggering of Large Earthquakes. *Nature Scientific Reports*, 4, 6100, DOI 10.1038/srep06100.

Nateghi-A, F. 1997. Seismic upgrade design of a low-rise steel building. *Engineering Structures*, 19(11), 954–63.

Nel, P. and M. Righarts. 2008. Natural disasters and the risk of violent civil conflict. *International Studies Quarterly*, 52: 159–85. DOI 10.1111/j.1468-2478.2007.00495.x.

Nelson, T. 2010a. When disaster strikes: on the relationship between natural disaster and interstate. *Global Change, Peace & Security*, 22(2), 155–74. DOI 10.1080/14781151003770788.

———. 2010b. Rejecting the gift horse: international politics of disaster aid refusal. *Conflict, Security & Development*, 10(3), 379–402. DOI 10.1080/14678802.2010.484202.

Neumayer, E. and T. Plümper. 2007. The Gendered Nature of Natural Disasters: The Impact of Catastrophic Events on the Gender Gap in Life Expectancy, 1981–2002. *Annals of the Association of American Geographers*, 97(3), 551–66. DOI 10.1111/j.1467-8306.2007.00563.x.

Newman, D. 1997. Conflicting Israeli peace discourses. *Peace Review*, 9(3), 417–24. DOI 10.1080/10402659708426086.

Nicholson, C.T.M. 2014. Climate change and the politics of causal reasoning: the case of climate change and migration. *The Geographical Journal*, 180, 151–60. DOI 10.1111/geoj.12062.

Nicolson, H.G. 1939. *Diplomacy*. New York: Harcourt Brace.

Nye, J. 1990. Bound to lead: *The changing nature of American power*. New York: Basic Books.

Nyong, A., F. Adesina, B. Osman Elasha. 2007. The value of indigenous knowledge in climate change mitigation and adaptation strategies in the African Sahel. *Mitigation and Adaptation Strategies for Global Change*, 12, 787–97. DOI 10.1007/s11027-007-9099-0.

Olsen, G.R., N. Carstensen, and K. Høyen. 2003. Humanitarian Crises: What Determines the Level of Emergency Assistance? Media Coverage, *Donor Interests and the Aid Business. Disasters*, 27(2), 109–26. DOI 10.1111/1467-7717.00223.

Olson, R.S. 2000. Toward a Politics of Disaster: Losses, Values, Agendas, and Blame. *International Journal of Mass Emergencies and Disasters*, 18(1), 265–87.

Olson, R.S. and A.C. Drury. 1997. Un-therapeutic communities: a cross-national analysis of post-disaster political unrest. *International Journal of Mass Emergencies and Disasters*, 15(2), 221–38.

OSSO and La Red. 2009. *DesInventar Disaster Inventory System: Methodological Guide Version 8.1.9*. La Red and OSSO, Colombia.

Park, J., T.-R. A. Song, J. Tromp, E. Okal, S. Stein, G. Roult, E. Clevede, G. Laske, H. Kanamori, P. Davis, J. Berger, C. Braitenberg, M. Van Camp, X. Lei, H. Sun, H. Xu, and S. Rossat. 2005. Earth's free oscillations excited by the 26 December 2004 Sumatra-Andaman earthquake. *Science*, 308(5725), 1139–44. DOI 10.1126/science.1112305.

Pelling, M. and K. Dill. 2010. Disaster politics: tipping points for change in the adaptation of sociopolitical regimes. *Progress in Human Geography*, 34(1), 21–37. DOI 10.1177/0309132509105004.

Perrow, C. 1998. *Normal Accidents*, 2nd edition. Princeton, NJ: Princeton University Press.

Rosen, A.M. 2015. The Wrong Solution at the Right Time: The Failure of the Kyoto Protocol on Climate Change. *Politics & Policy*, 43(1), 30–58. DOI 10.1111/polp.12105.

Roy, A.G. 2012. *The magic of Bollywood: at home and abroad*. Wallingford: CABI.

Roy, P., V. Priyanka, M.K. Goel, and S. Rasania. 2014. Measles Eradication: Issues, Strategies and Challenges. *Journal of Communicable Diseases*, 46(3), 25–28.

Rudge, J. and R. Gilchrist. 2005. Excess winter morbidity among older people at risk of cold homes: a population-based study in a London borough. *Journal of Public Health*, 27(4), 353–58. DOI 10.1093/pubmed/fdi051.

Segalla, S.D. 2012. The 1959 Moroccan oil poisoning and US Cold War disaster diplomacy. *The Journal of North African Studies*, 17(2), 315–36. DOI 10.1080/13629387.2011.610118.

Silverstein, M.E. 1991. 'International disaster research', paper presented at International Telemedicine/Disaster Medicine Conference, National Aeronautics and Space Administration. *American Institute of Aeronautics and Astronautics*, Bethesda, MD, 9–11 December.

Spence, R. 2004. Risk and regulation: can improved government action reduce the impacts of natural disasters? *Building Research and Information*, 32(5), 391–402. DOI 10.1080/0961321042000221043.

Stone, R. 2013. Sizing Up a Slumbering Giant. *Science*, 341, 1060–61.

Streich, P.A. and D.B. Mislan. 2014. What follows the storm? Research on the effect of disasters on conflict and cooperation. *Global Change, Peace & Security*, 26(1), 55–70.

Terry, F. 2002. *Condemned to Repeat? The Paradox of Humanitarian Action*. Ithaca, NY: Cornell University Press.

Twigg, J. 1999–2000. The age of accountability?: Future community involvement in disaster reduction. *Australian Journal of Emergency Management*, 14(4), 51–58.

UNISDR. 2005. Hyogo framework for action 2005–2015: *Building the resilience of nations and communities to disasters*. Geneva: UNISDR (United Nations Office for Disaster Risk Reduction).

———. 2009. Information from http://www.unisdr.org/we/inform/terminology UNISDR (United Nations Office for Disaster Risk Reduction). Last accessed 3 August 2015.

———. 2015. *Sendai Framework for Disaster Risk Reduction* 2015–2030. Geneva: UNISDR (United Nations Office for Disaster Risk Reduction).

Urbainczyk, T. 2008. *Slave Revolts in Antiquity*. Berkeley and Los Angeles: University of California Press.

USGS. 2015. Information from http://earthquake.usgs.gov/earthquakes/eqinthenews/2004/us2004slav/faq.php and http://earthquake.usgs.gov/earthquakes/eqinthenews/2004/us2004slav USGS (United States Geological Survey), Menlo Park, California. Last accessed 2 August 2015.

Van Belle, D.A. 2003. Bureaucratic Responsiveness to the News Media: Comparing the Influence of *The New York Times* and Network Television News Coverage on US Foreign Aid Allocations. *Political Communication*, 20(3), 263–85. DOI 10.1080/10584600390218896.

Vermaak, J. and D. van Niekerk. 2004. Disaster risk reduction initiatives in South Africa. *Development Southern Africa*, 21(3), 555–74. DOI 10.1080/0376835042000265487.

Waage, J. and C. Yap (eds.) 2015. *Thinking Beyond Sectors for Sustainable Development*. London: Ubiquity Press.

Warnaar, M. 2013. Shaken, Not Stirred: Iran's Foreign Relations and the 2003 Bam Earthquake. Chapter 11, pp. 238–67 in S.R. Sensarma and A. Sarkar (eds.), *Disaster Risk Management: Conflict and Cooperation*, Concept Publishing, New Delhi.

Weldon, J. 2010. Forgotten Namesake: The Illinois Good Samaritan Act's Inexcusable Failure to Provide Immunity to Non-Medical Rescuers. *The John Marshall Law Review*, 43(4), 1097–1118.

WHO. 2007. *Definitions: emergencies*. Geneva: WHO (World Health Organization).

Wisner, B., P. Blaikie., T. Cannon, and I. Davis. 2004. *At Risk: Natural Hazards: People's Vulnerability and Disasters*, 2nd edition. London: Routledge.

Wisner, B., J.C. Gaillard, and I. Kelman (eds.) 2012. *Handbook of Hazards and Disaster Risk Reduction*. Abingdon: Routledge.

Wyss, M. and S. Peppoloni (eds.) 2015. *Geoethics: Ethical Challenges and Case Studies in Earth Sciences*. Philadelphia, PA: Elsevier.

Yim, E.S., D.W. Callaway, S. Fares, and G.R. Ciottone. 2009a. Disaster Diplomacy: Current Controversies and Future Prospects. *Prehospital and Disaster Medicine*, 24(4), 291–93.

Yim, E.S., R.Y. Choi, and M.J. Van Rooyen. 2009b. Maintaining Health Sector Collaborations between United States Non-Governmental Organizations and North Korea through Innovation and Planning. *Prehospital and Disaster Medicine*, 24(3), 153–60. DOI 10.1017/S1049023X00006750.

Yim, E.S. and M.J. Van Rooyen. 2009c. Health and Disaster Diplomacy in North Korea: Ensuring Access and Accountability in Complex Political Environments. *Prehospital and Disaster Medicine*, 24(4), 294–96.

Zaharna, R.S., A. Arsenault, and A. Fisher (eds.) 2014. *Relational, Networked and Collaborative Approaches to Public Diplomacy: The Connective Mindshift*. Abingdon: Routledge.

www.ingramcontent.com/pod-product-compliance
Lightning Source LLC
Chambersburg PA
CBHW031333230926
51848CB00001B/210
* 9 7 8 9 0 0 4 3 1 6 1 3 3 *